100
GREATS

IRELAND'S
100 CRICKET GREATS

100 GREATS

IRELAND'S
100 CRICKET GREATS

COMPILED BY
GERARD SIGGINS AND JAMES FITZGERALD

NONSUCH

First published 2006

Nonsuch Publishing
73 Lower Leeson Street
Dublin 2
Ireland

www.nonsuch-publishing.com

© Gerard Siggins & James Fitzgerald, 2006

The right of Gerard Siggins & James Fitzgerald to be identified
as the Authors of this work has been asserted in accordance
with the Copyrights, Designs and Patents Act 1988.

British Library Cataloguing in Publication Data.
A catalogue record for this book is available from the British Library.

ISBN 1 84588 564 3
ISBN-13 (from January 2007) 978 1 84588 564 9

Typesetting and origination by Tempus Publishing Limited.
Printed in Great Britain.

Introduction

It seems that cricket, more than most sports, is given to comparing players of different eras in an effort to find out who is the greatest of all-time. How would WG Grace have fared against the bowling skills of Michael Holding? How would the so-called invincible Australian team that toured England in 1948 with Bradman, Lindwall and Miller compare to their modern-day counterparts with Ponting, Warne and McGrath? And who is the greatest wicketkeeper of all time? We can – and do – argue these points fruitlessly without definitive conclusion but in many ways the fun is in the discussion and debate rather than any aspiration to arrive at a consensus.

And so it is for this book. There are some players, Bob Lambert, Lucius Gwynn, Jimmy Boucher, Alec O'Riordan, Dermott Monteith, Ivan Anderson and Ed Joyce for example who no one could construct a reasonable argument for exclusion from a book containing the 100 best Irish cricketers. But we will admit that some of those who made the final list could easily have been left out in favour of others who did not. Ultimately it came down to a combination of statistical review and subjective opinion and we are happy to accept that other observers may disagree wildly with our choices.

We used several criteria to decide upon our final 100 – and the 'First XI'. The players had to have played for Ireland so this excludes a number who dominated domestic cricket but for one reason or another never got the nod at the higher level. It also excludes the likes of Martin McCague and Tom Horan, Irishmen by birth who went on to play Test cricket for England and Australia but who had no real connection with the game on this island. And it also excludes a series of top-class players who turned out a few times for Ireland as guest overseas players but who could never in any conventional sense of the word be described as Irish cricketers. As such, Steve Waugh, Mark Waugh, Hansie Cronje, Jonty Rhodes and Shahid Afridi may well get into a book about the 100 best players from Australia, South Africa or Pakistan but they do not get into this one, save a cursory mention in the introduction.

That said, there are players included in these pages who did not grow up or learn this great game in Ireland. There have been several fine players who arrived on these shores as young men, already adept at cover drive or leg cutter, and eventually played for Ireland. The likes of Australian-born Trent Johnston and Jeremy Bray, Englishmen Charles Lawrence and Leslie Kidd, South African Andre Botha or Pakistani Alf Masood have all been included because they made Ireland their home, settled here, qualified to play and were committed to the concept that is Irish cricket. To be honest, their eligibility was never in doubt for us.

By way of a disclaimer, we predict that there will be many perfectly reasonable arguments presented to us upon the publication of this book as to why one player got in ahead of another. This is not a list that has been carved in stone and handed down to us by the cricket god but rather a group of players chosen following reference to all available records, reports and other information about the game since the first international match was played here in 1855. We have also been indebted to the contributions, advice and suggestions from a number of people who know far more about the game in Ireland than we do.

Derek Scott was never selected to play cricket for Ireland but if there was a book about the people who had helped shape, develop and record for posterity the game in this country, Scotty would be at the very top. His detailed records, statistics and other information have been invaluable to us, but more importantly he has also given us free access to tap into the various files and databases he keeps in his head. Having served as assistant honorary secretary from 1954-1974, honorary secretary from 1974-1997 and president of the Irish Cricket Union in 2001, he is truly a giant of the game in this country. And we are very grateful to him for giving his time and neatly compiled records so freely and enthusiastically.

There have been many others who have been generous in their help. In the course of our research we pored over many written records, newspaper clippings, radio interviews and magazine articles and as such we are grateful to the many writers on the game in Ireland over the last century and a half, whether they be the professional scribes such as the late Sean Pender, Stanley Bergin, Paul McWeeney and Karl Johnston, Ian Callender, Philip Boylan, Peter Breen, Emmet Riordan, Peter O'Reilly, Robin Walsh, Carl Anderson and Robert Fenton, or the indefatigable chroniclers who compiled the histories of the clubs and unions. Prime among these are the books by Pat Hone, Clarence Hiles, Billy Platt, Michael Milne, Dermott Monteith, Michael Halliday and Gerard Siggins, but also many club publications that help fill in the gaps of our knowledge of Irish cricket.

Perhaps the finest cricket website in the world is run by a couple of Irishmen and the existence of www.cricketeurope.org has made our life a lot easier. In addition, John Elder and Barry Chambers have given freely and cheerfully of their own time to help us with this book and we are very grateful for that. Their statistics, compiled by John Boomer and Gerry Byrne, are a fabulous resource.

During the research stages of this book we contacted several former and current players and administrators to comment on their own careers or those of their peers. Without exception, they were delighted to help us and it has been a great insight for us to talk to those who have seen the higher levels of the game up close either on the field of play or in the committee room. As such, we would like to thank Roy Harrison, Ivan Anderson, Jeremy Bray, Kyle McCallan, Alan Lewis, Deryck Vincent, Joe Doherty, Michael Sharp, Mary Sharp, David Williams, Adrian Birrell, Gerry Duffy, Roy Torrens, John Elder, Paul Mooney, Peter Gillespie, Brian Buttimer, Fergus Carroll, Gerry Byrne, Simon Corlett and Murray Power for their invaluable contributions.

Several people have helped us at various stages in the production of this book, helping to root out all the nasty errors in fact, spelling or grammar that we did not spot. For that reason, Derek Scott, Murray Power, Daniel Payne (Leicestershire) and Karien Jonckheere must be thanked but it should be pointed out that the errors and omissions of this book are the fault exclusively of us, the authors.

James Fitzgerald would also like to thank sports editor of *The Irish Times* Malachy Logan for giving him the opportunity to write regularly about Irish cricket (and even paying him to do so). Malachy's ongoing commitment has been a part of the continued development of Irish cricket. I would also like to thank my parents, Ray and Joy, the rest of my family and friends, whose ongoing love and encouragement are a genuine source of inspiration. And to Siggins, a veteran of several excellent books, for shepherding me to my debut.

Gerard Siggins would like to thank the *Sunday Tribune* editor Noirin Hegarty and sports editor PJ Cunningham for their encouragement and indulgence in this project and in allowing me to be distracted from my real job so I could write about cricket. The love and support of Martha, Jack, Lucy, Billy and Danny the Dachshund is a constant blessing and I thank them for their help on this book.

But thanks most of all to the 656 men who have played this great game in the Irish colours. We are sorry we had to omit the majority of you, but please be assured your names and your deeds will be long remembered and valued.

James Fitzgerald
Gerard Siggins
September, 2006

100 Club Greats

IJ Anderson
O Andrews
RJ Barnes
GF Barry
JDR Benson
SF Bergin
GFH Berkeley
AC Botha
JC Boucher
JP Bray
FH Browning
Rev. J Byrne
MF Cohen
OD Colhoun
AD Comyn
G Cooke
SC Corlett
D Cronin
JD Curry
PJ Davy
TH Dixon
B Donaghey
GA Duffy
AR Dunlop
J Dunn
MD Dwyer
RL Eagleson
JWG Elder
F Fee
JB Ganly
PG Gillespie
DE Goodwin
WR Gregory
LH Gwynn

M Halliday
BB Hamilton
WD Hamilton
W Harrington
GD Harrison
J Harrison
D Heasley
JG Heaslip
CJ Hoey
L Hone
SSJ Huey
JW Hynes
E Ingram
PB Jackson
TO Jameson
CL Johnson
DT Johnston
DI Joyce
EC Joyce
AP Kelly
GWFB Kelly
FG Kempster
EL Kidd
R Lamba
RH Lambert
C Lawrence
DA Lewis
J Macdonald
TJ Macdonald
NC Mahony
H Martin
MA Masood
A McBrine
WK McCallan

AGAM McCoubrey
P McCrum
A McFarlane
TG McVeagh
JM Meldon
JAM Molins
JD Monteith
PJK Mooney
EJG Morgan
Hon. HGH Mulholland
AN Nelson
BA O'Brien
NJ O'Brien
Sir Timothy O'Brien
AJ O'Riordan
MW Patterson
AF Penny
JS Pollock
W Pollock
JA Prior
MP Rea
MS Reith
TC Ross
EDR Shearer
JF Short
SG Smyth
RG Torrens
DN Trotter
DA Vincent
L Warke
SJS Warke
AR White

First XI in bold.

Born: 13 August 1944, Armagh

Batting

Mts	Inns	NOs	Runs
86	141	25	3,777
Avg	50s	100s	Cts
32.56	13	7	40

Bowling

O	M	R	W
481	151	1,277	48
Avg	5WI	10WM	
26.60	1	-	

Highest score: 198 not out v Canada, Toronto 1973

Best bowling: 5-21 v Scotland, Ayr 1974

Ivan Anderson was arguably the most complete Irish cricketer in history and certainly one of the few players of his time who was capable of playing county cricket. A forceful, stylish right-hand batsman, swooping cover fielder and niggardly off-spin bowler, Anderson became a legend of the Ulster club scene during a wonderful forty-year career and also broke records at international level, some of which still stand to this day.

His tally of seven centuries is the most by an Irishman, three more than the next contenders. His highest score of 198 not out against Canada in Toronto remains the highest individual score for Ireland in any type of match. And he is the only Irish player to score centuries in both innings of a match, a feat he achieved against Scotland at Glasgow in 1976.

Born in the city of Armagh, Anderson's talent was spotted at an early age. He played for the Royal School Armagh and also represented Ulster Schools, Ulster Colts, Irish Schools and later, Queen's University Belfast, Ulster Country and finally, as a twenty-one-year-old in 1966, he made his debut for Ireland against Fred Titmus's

Middlesex. He top scored in both innings of that losing match at Ormeau, Belfast, a sign of things to come.

Once he left university, Anderson returned to his club in Armagh but in 1969 he moved to Lisburn and, being friendly with some of the Waringstown members, he decided to switch clubs. The family atmosphere of Waringstown made it a more attractive place for the newly married Anderson.

'At that time, Waringstown had a good team, having won the NCU Challenge Cup in the previous two years and the senior league two years earlier. Ivan helped to make them a great team,' wrote Clarence Hiles in *A History of Senior Cricket in Ulster*. In all he appeared in fifteen NCU cup finals, winning all of them and he continued to play to a high standard long after most of his contemporaries had given up. In the 1993 NCU cup final, aged forty-nine, he bowled 22 overs finishing with figures of 2-30.

Throughout the late 1960s and 1970s, Anderson was the mainstay of Ireland's batting line-up. He scored the first of his seven tons in just his sixth match, 110 not out against the Combined Services at Aldershot, and the following year took over the captaincy from Ireland and Lions rugby international Raymond Hunter.

Perhaps he was too young at the time (not quite twenty-four years old) and he did not have a particularly successful period in his short spell as captain of Ireland. Mind you, his first two games in charge were against Bill Lawry's Australians, which predictably enough yielded two defeats. His three subsequent games brought a win against the Combined Services and two draws, with Scotland and the MCC. But Anderson did not always see eye to eye with selectors and the following 1969 season Dougie Goodwin of Malahide was appointed captain and Anderson's fleeting chance as leader was gone.

By his high standards and for someone so talented, Anderson went through a little downturn in form in the following seasons and it is no secret that selectors were becoming concerned about his place in the team. The tour to the USA and Canada in 1973 restored their faith and his knock of 198 not out remains a record (both for Ireland and for any player against Canada). Being left stranded two short of what would have been a historic double century is a cross that he will always have to bear (as will John Elder, the number eleven batsman who was given out lbw before Anderson could reach the milestone).

'I don't think he ever forgave me,' joked Elder recently. 'But Ivan was a magnificent bat and unequalled as a cover fielder. Nobody has ever batted better for Ireland against real quality bowling than Ivan,' said Elder.

'Of course I forgave him,' says Anderson, who scored 100 of those runs in a single session. 'Maybe I didn't forgive the umpire though because the ball was clearly going over the top of the stumps... The innings was just one of those things. The first ball I faced took a leap off the pitch, took my outside edge and flew over the slips. I think the next chance I gave was at about 120 but it might have all ended with a first baller,' he said.

Anderson was a player who always received the respect of his opponents, even when they

were county or Test players. Visiting professionals usually rated him as the best cricketer they faced in Ireland. According to former Ireland teammate and captain Michael Halliday, in a two-day match against the MCC at Lord's in 1977, Ivan was denied two centuries in the same match by the South African Clive Rice, who bowled two overs of bouncers to prevent an Irish win and Ivan's second century.

'Ivan would have been good enough to grace any county ground,' said Halliday.

While he was a batsman first and foremost, he was a much under-rated slow bowler, often being over-looked at a time when Ireland was generally blessed in the bowling department with the likes of Alec O'Riordan and Goodwin and with quality slow bowlers in particular, like Halliday and Dermott Monteith. But there was a time when Anderson's bowling actually kept him in the team. Coming into the three-day game against Scotland at Ayr, Anderson was going through a rare loss of form with the bat and even though he had scored that record-breaking knock of 198 not out the previous year, his place was in jeopardy.

Ivan John Anderson
continued

In a low-scoring match he managed just three and a duck and by the third day, it looked a dead cause for Ireland as the Scots put on 53 for the first wicket, needing just 146 for victory. At tea, the selectors sat down and picked their team for the next game, a three-day match against Wales two weeks later. Although he didn't know it at the time, Anderson was to be left out but a remarkable feat of bowling made the selectors hastily reconsider.

On a turning pitch he combined with Dermott Monteith to remove the entire Scottish batting line-up for just 93, some 52 runs short.

Anderson took career-best figures of 5-21 off 19 overs and Monteith managed 5-29 off 24.4 to register a memorable victory for the Irish.

Known affectionately as the Goat due to his trademark beard that turned progressively whiter as the years went on, Anderson was an exceptional cricketer and one who would have dominated any era he happened to be born in. Picking an all-time Ireland eleven is always a precarious and argument-inspiring pursuit but including the name of IJ Anderson high on the batting line-up will never spark any response other than a vigorous nod of agreement.

Oscar Andrews
RHB, RM; North Down, North of Ireland CC and Ireland (1902-09)

Born: 24 July 1876, West Derby, Liverpool
Died: 30 October 1956, Belfast

Batting

Mts	Inns	NOs	Runs
8	15	2	139
Avg	50s	100s	Cts
10.69	-	-	7

Bowling

O	M	R	W
31	7	107	4
Avg	5WI	10WM	
26.75	-	-	

Highest score: 41 v I Zingari, Vice-Regal Lodge, 1906
Best bowling: 2-8 v London County, Crystal Palace, 1902

Oscar Andrews was a member of a celebrated County Down family that not only produced cricket and hockey internationals, but a Northern Ireland prime minister, deputy prime minister, a lord chief justice and the builder of the *RMS Titanic*.

Educated at Rossall School in Lancashire, Oscar made his debut for North Down at the age of fifteen in the 1891 Junior Cup Final, two years later graduating to the senior side. Although he played occasionally for North of Ireland from 1893 (he made 148* v Pembroke in 1898), his main allegiance was to the Comber club until 1900 when he moved to North of Ireland in Belfast. From then up to the First World War, North won the Challenge Cup nine times and were league champions on seven occasions, with Andrews captain from 1902-19. According to the club history 'there is little doubt that this success was, in a large part, attributable to one man'.

North's records are incomplete, but they show Andrews scored over 12,500 runs, with at least 13 centuries, and a top score of 186. As a bowler he took in the region of 1,500 wickets, taking 100 wickets every season from 1901-05. In the fifteen seasons before the war he topped the club batting averages thirteen times and the bowling averages eleven times.

He won cup medals with North Down in 1893, 1894 (with Holywood needing 56 to win Andrews took 4-13 and Willie Turner 6-12 to bowl them out 22 short) and 1897 (when he made 73 and 100 in the final). In all he played in 13 cup finals, winning 11. His best bowling, 9-44, came against Ulster in the 1912 final, with 5-17 in the first innings.

His best season with the ball was 1902, when he took 112 wickets at 7.7. His best with the bat was 1911, when he made 1,508 runs and put on a partnership of 161 with Willie Pollock in forty-five minutes against Phoenix.

While his club performances are legendary, his Ireland record is only mediocre. It was unfortunately blighted by the anti-northern bias of the times, and all but one of his eight caps came on two tours, to England in 1902 and North America in 1909, on both of which he was the only Ulsterman. However, it appears he was also lukewarm about playing for Ireland and declared himself unavailable on many occasions when selected.

He was first picked in 1901 against South Africa, but when the NCU objected to Phoenix organising the fixture and selecting the team, Andrews withdrew. The following season he went on Sir Tim O'Brien's tour, his best scores being 29* against London County and 23* against Cambridge. Later that summer he made a brilliant 103 for the NCU against Leinster in the interprovincial. He also toured the US and Canada with Frank Browning's team, but made just 13 runs in six innings in the cap matches.

Andrews was known as 'the Champion Cricketer' and was quite the well-rounded player: a dashing, punishing batsman, a focused pace bowler who attacked the stumps and an inspirational leader. He was also a noted hockey player, winning four caps from 1889-98. His cousin Willie Andrews was capped once at cricket in 1928.

100
GREATS

Rev. Robert James Barnes

LHB, RLB; Dublin University, Armagh, Waringstown, Ireland (1928-47)

In 1928, the *Cricketer* magazine wrote about a seventeen-year-old schoolboy: 'A most promising all-rounder is R J Barnes, of Armagh, who made 73 against Munster, and who has some useful scores to his credit in Ulster cricket this season'. Bobby Barnes followed this in the interprovincial against Leinster when, batting No.8, he top scored with 32 out of 144. He was elevated to the Irish side against MCC at Ormeau and made 9 in his first innings. It was a breakneck summer for the talented sportsman from the Royal School, Armagh.

He made sporadic Ireland appearances over the next five seasons, when he was studying at Trinity. For the club he was a prolific scorer, making an unbeaten century against Manchester University in 1932 and a club record 182 against Merrion in the cup in 1937. The following season he watched them being beaten from the non-striker's end as Billy Mellon made 203* and Barnes 130 in a stand of 227 against Pembroke. He made 1,423 runs for the university, reaching 1,000 in just 29 innings. His 14 competitive fifties is still a club record.

Rev. Robert James Barnes
continued

Born: 25 March 1911, Armagh
Died: 12 March 1987, Belfast

Batting

Mts	Inns	NOs	Runs
14	24	2	433
Avg	**50s**	**100s**	**Cts**
19.68	2	-	10

Bowling

O	M	R	W
82	17	203	13
Avg	**5WI**	**10WM**	
15.66	-	-	

Highest score: 59 v Yorkshire, Ormeau, 1949
Best bowling: 4-18 v Scotland, Greenock, 1946

After top scoring in both innings with 44 and 48 against MCC at College Park in 1932 (and taking 2-31 in 20 overs), he didn't play for Ireland for five years. He returned for four games in 1937 in which he never passed 13.

On graduation in 1939 he was appointed curate to the parish of Donaghcloney, which included the cricketing hotbed of Waringstown. He continued to score heavily for the club, making centuries against Muckamore and North Down in 1942 and winning Challenge Cup medals in 1943 and 1944. One day at the Lawn the scoreboard recorded that he had made 100, and the applause was great when he was out immediately afterwards. Unfortunately the scoreboard was wrong and he had only made 99. It was typical Barnes' character that he was the least upset person on the ground. He captained he club for six seasons in the 1940s. One of his most celebrated innings was an unbeaten 101 for the NCU against North-West in August 1947.

Barnes was recalled when Ireland resumed after the war and made several important contributions. At Greenock in 1946 he made 48 and then routed the Scots with 12-3-18-4. His bat-

ting was the key to the great win over the 1947 South Africans, who were routed by Boucher for 114. It was a one-day 'time' match, so a first innings lead was usually enough to win, but Ireland collapsed to 36-4 when Barnes – who had been called up as a late substitute – joined Donald Shearer. Barnes made 57 as the pair secured the crucial lead and a famous victory.

In the remarkable finish to the 1948 game against Yorkshire, Ireland set off to chase 410 in two sessions – and with Barnes crashing a rapid 59, were all out ten minutes after tea for 248.

His bowling was used sparingly by Ireland, but his right-arm leg breaks took 13 wickets at 15.6. He was devastating in club cricket and took 5-10 and 6-27 for Trinity against Queen's in 1938.

Barnes was also a good rugby player and marked his only international cap, against Wales in 1933, with a try as Ireland won 10-5. Bobby played alongside his brother Jackie on the latter's debut against New Zealand in 1937. It was a lethal pitch and the game finished in one day, with Jackie making a pair. The younger brother was killed in a RAF training accident during the war.

George Frith Barry
Leinster, Vice-Regal, Phoenix and Ireland (1858-77)

Born: Buttevant, County Cork (date unknown)
Died: Rathmines, Dublin circa 1891 (aged 54)

Batting

Mts	Inns	NOs	Runs
22	39	1	304
Avg	100s	50s	Cts
8.00	-	-	11

Bowling

O	M	R	W
n/a	n/a	217	19
Avg	5WI	10WM	
11.42	-	-	

These bowling figures only apply to games for which analyses survive. Barry bowled in two other games, taking a wicket in each at unknown cost.

Highest innings: 43 v I Zingari, Vice-Regal Ground, 1860
Best bowling: 4-10 v All England XI, Rathmines 1869

George Frith Barry was one of the most remarkable cricketers of the nineteenth century, a founder member of the Leinster club who captained the club for thirty-four years. A tough batsman and useful bowler, he played twenty-two times for Ireland over nineteen years and captained the side on at least ten occasions. He was a lucky captain if nothing else, winning nine of the ten tosses, and his record reads a respectable three wins, four draws and three defeats.

Born in Cork, his family moved to Dublin when he was very young and he joined in with the new sporting craze of cricket when a club was set up in Rathmines. He was fortunate that the Earl of Carlisle, then the Lord Lieutenant, was casting about for cricketers to pack his Vice-Regal side and was able to offer lucrative jobs for likely lads. The Earl 'took Barry under his wing' as well as finding him a 'substantial berth in the State Paper Department of the Castle'. He rewarded the Earl with a big fifty on his debut for Vice-Regal.

Quiet and unassuming in manner, he possessed steel when he needed it. There was a celebrated dispute between Leinster and Phoenix when the latter pulled a fast one. Phoenix fielded with eleven men, with no mention that one was a substitute, but when they came to bat along came a crack Trinity player, David Trotter (qv), who went in and made a big score. Barry held his tongue but when Trotter later left the ground he refused to allow Phoenix a fielding substitute and a serious argument ensued. Both sides walked off and the game was abandoned. Barry, also a member of Phoenix, took no further part in that club's activities.

Ireland played only twenty-six games from 1858-77, but Barry played in twenty-two of them, all but two in Dublin. He made his debut, opening the batting, against Birkenhead Park but made just 0 and 1. He made 28 – a good score in those days of dire pitches – the following season against I Zingari, but his best innings was against the same team in 1860. Barry made 43 in the second innings and was presented with a new bat by the visitors in token of their 'admiration of his splendid play'.

He bowled in fewer than half his internationals, but was a useful contributor. In 1869 he took 2-29 and 4-10 off 16 overs against a strong All England XI, and later that summer took 2-21 and 3-15 against I Zingari.

A teammate, Arthur Samuels, wrote that, 'At one time, one of the best all round cricketers in Ireland. He could bat, bowl, or field as well as, or better than, most men, and he makes a first-rate captain of an eleven'.

His brother, Sam, won four Irish caps from 1859-62. George was a leading chess player of his day, and took part in a famous game, against GB Fraser in the UK International in 1888, which was ranked in the top 50 of all time in a recent book. His obituary described him as 'a boy up to the day he died... the idol and pet of the whole cricketing community'.

Justin David Ramsay Benson
RHB, RAM; Malahide, Leicestershire and Ireland (1993-97)

100 GREATS

Born: 1 March 1967, Dublin

Batting

Mts	Inns	NOs	Runs
59	60	7	1,528
Avg	**50s**	**100s**	**Cts**
28.83	9	-	32

Bowling

O	M	R	W
86.2	5	477	17
Avg	**5WI**	**10WM**	
28.06	-	-	

Highest score: 79 v Netherlands, Svanholm Brondby 1996
Best bowling: 3-45 v Middlesex, Castle Avenue 1997

Although born in Dublin, Justin Benson grew up in England and would probably never have pulled on the Irish sweater but for the fact that he never really established himself at county level for Leicestershire. In the six years he was on the books at Grace Road he played 56 matches, scoring four centuries at an average of 28.

In 1993 it became clear that he would be available to play for Ireland in the ICC Trophy the following February although he was still a Leicestershire player. He made his full Ireland debut against the touring Australians at Castle Avenue in July 1993, opening the batting and scoring just one run as Ireland were rolled over for just 89.

He didn't play again for Ireland until the ICC Trophy in Kenya where he really established himself in the side.

While Ireland did not blow the competition away in that tournament, Benson impressed, finishing up as the team's top-scorer with 235 runs at an average of 39.16 including a fine innings of 73 not out against Malaysia at Simba Union Cricket Club in Nairobi. On being released by Leicestershire he came to Ireland to play club cricket with Malahide in 1995 and had an outstanding season, breaking the records for most runs in a season and most 100s in a season in Leinster cricket. He scored a total of 1,221 runs for Malahide that season at an average of a mite over 61 and a top score of 160.

But while he was a bully at club level, he never really dominated bowling in the same way at international level and was sometimes accused of being a lazy cricketer. Clearly a very talented shot-maker and technician, the fact that he never scored a century for Ireland in 60 innings damages his legacy. He hit a fine 74 not out in a rain-affected draw against the West Indies at Castle Avenue in 1995 when he and Stephen Smyth (98 not out) were left stranded before they could get to three figures.

In 1996, he took over from the injured Alan Lewis as captain of Ireland and led the country to its first ever win of the Triple Crown series (against Scotland, Wales and England Amateurs) and followed it up with victory in the inaugural European Championships, held in Denmark. In the final of that competition he made 79 to ensure that Ireland passed the Netherlands' total of 223. It was to be his highest score for Ireland and it won him the man of the match award that day in Brondby.

He was retained as captain for the 1997 ICC Trophy in Malaysia and brought the side to within eight runs of making it to the 1999 World Cup finals in England. But that narrow defeat to Kenya in the semi-final and a disappointing finish against Scotland in the third-place playoff meant Ireland would have to wait another ten years before they finally got to play in the world's premier knock-out tournament.

Benson retired at the end of that season, finishing in style with a half-century against the MCC at Lord's. As captain his 48 per cent win rate (in twenty-nine appearances) is bettered only by Jason Molins and his overall record is more than respectable with a batting average of almost 30. He also took 17 wickets at 28 including 3-45 in the famous 1997 Benson & Hedges Cup win over Middlesex at Castle Avenue, a spell that included the scalp of former England captain Mike Gatting.

Stanley Francis Bergin

LHB; Pembroke and Ireland (1949-65)

Born: 18 December 1926, Dublin
Died: 4 August 1969, Dublin

Batting

Mts	Inns	NOs	Runs
53	98	7	2524
Avg	50s	100s	Cts
27.74	15	2	17

Highest score: 137 v Scotland, College Park 1959

Stanley Bergin was Ireland's opening batsman for sixteen years, missing just seven matches in that time. It was an era of poor pitches and that he emerged with an average as high as 27.74 indicates his quality. His obituary in *Wisden* – he died suddenly, aged forty-two – asserts that 'If he had chosen to do so, there is little doubt that he could have held his own in County cricket'.

One of a family of six boys, Stanley was educated at Westland Row CBS, a school celebrated for Gaelic games. He played football and hurling for the school and represented Leinster at college level. He was also a top junior-soccer player and played fullback for Monkstown in rugby's Leinster Senior Cup. Add to that a golf handicap of 15 and league-level table tennis and you have a remarkable all-round sportsman. But on top of it all was his love and aptitude for the game of cricket.

He joined Pembroke, for whom his brother Bernard opened the batting. Bernard won two caps for Ireland against the 1937 New Zealanders, when the three-day match ended in one day. Two other brothers, Gus (Railway Union) and Gerry (Pembroke) also played senior cricket.

Stanley was only fourteen when he made his first XI debut in a side sporting several internationals, including the Williams brothers. A small, wiry batsman who always wore glasses, Bergin was particularly strong square of the wicket, but the hallmark of his game was his concentration. This was best seen against the 1951 South Africans, who fielded Cuan McCarthy, the fastest bowler in the world at the time. Ireland lost by an innings, but Bergin batted through the second innings for an unbeaten 79 (out of 130) – the last time an Irish batsman carried his bat. He was similarly dogged in batting for six hours against Leicestershire in 1959 for innings of 31 and 23. Among his other notable feats for Ireland were four consecutive fifties in 1950-51.

He made 7,713 runs with Pembroke before he retired from cricket altogether in 1965. His career average of 36.9 was the record when he quit, and is still good enough to make the top ten all-time LCU batsmen. He won the Marchant Cup for the province's leading batsman on four occasions and won league and cup doubles with the club in 1944, 1946, 1954 and 1957, the last as captain. He made eight centuries for Pembroke, the first an unbeaten 101 against Merrion at the age of sixteen.

A journalist by trade, he was cricket correspondent for *The Irish Times* and the *Evening Herald*, and also wrote about Gaelic games. In those days of 'The Ban', his name used to appear in cricket scorecards as 'B Stanley' to preserve his reputation among the Gaels. He suffered a cricket ban too, in 1960, for accepting an individual award from Caltex, the forerunner of the Texaco awards. Since then only Dermott

Monteith (1971 and 1973) and Ed Joyce (2005) have won the award.

His two centuries for Ireland came against Scotland in 1959 and 1961, while he also made 69 and 63★ against Yorkshire in 1959. The 1961 hundred came in Cork, where he took more than six hours. It took him half an hour to get from 92 to 96 but he then began slashing wildly and was dropped twice. He never made a century at Lord's but came close in 1963 (88) and 1965 (78). His last game for Ireland was in September 1965 at Clontarf, close to where he lived. Several of his sons continued the cricketing tradition in Castle Avenue after his untimely death and Brendan represented North Leinster in the 1980s.

---

100 GREATS ——————————— **George Fitz-Hardinge Berkeley**
RHB, LAM; Oxford University, Cork County and Ireland (1890-91)

George Berkeley played only twice for Ireland but his actions off the field had an enormous impact on the country – and on the world as a whole. He had a most successful debut for Ireland, taking 7-20 against I Zingari in the Phoenix Park in 1890, and his first-class debut for Oxford was even more stellar, taking 8-70 against the 1890 Australians.

Born in Dublin, Berkeley was educated at Wellington College in England, where he was in the first eleven for four years. He went up to Oxford, where he won blues in each of his four years there. He excelled in the Varsity match, taking 27 wickets against Cambridge at less than 13.

He made an immediate mark at Oxford, stunning the Australians, although the students lost by an innings. 'The colonials found his deliveries little to their liking' wrote *Cricket* magazine, as Berkeley returned figures of 36.3-12-70-8. He played thirty-one more first-class games but never bettered that analysis. He was selected for the Gentlemen v the Players in 1892 but failed to make an impact.

Berkeley was also involved in a farcical situation during the Varsity match which led to a change in the laws of the game. Oxford's captain, Lionel Palairet, decided that it might be better to follow on, which was mandatory in those days. Under orders, Berkeley threw his wicket away, but the batsmen that followed were less subtle in their attempts and the Cambridge captain twigged what was going on and proceeded to bowl several wides to ensure Palairet's plan was foiled.

Berkeley had returned to Ireland after his first season at Oxford and was playing with Cork County when he was selected for Ireland against I Zingari in August. Described by Pat Hone as 'a left-hand bowler with a beautiful action', he bowled throughout from one end, taking 18-8-20-7 as IZ collapsed to 79 all out. Ireland made 109 and IZ 135 second time around (Berkeley 25-9-55-4) before Ireland crawled to 106-7 (Berkeley 5 not out) to win by three wickets.

I Zingari were Ireland's only opponents for the next four summers and Berkeley only played once more. The following year the

Born: 29 January 1870, Dublin
Died: 14 November 1955, Hanwell Castle, Banbury, Oxfordshire

Batting

Mts	Inns	NOs	Runs
2	3	1	8
Avg	50s	100s	Cts
4.00	-	-	4

Bowling

O	M	R	W
78	36	132	14
Avg	5WI	10WM	
9.43	1	1	

Highest score: 5* v I Zingari, Phoenix Park, 1890
Best bowling: 7-20 v I Zingari, Phoenix Park, 1890

match was drawn, with the Oxford student taking 3-25.

He played thirty-two first class games in all, taking 131 wickets at 20.75. His best bowling was that debut 8-70. He played occasionally thereafter for Cork County and Oxfordshire.

Berkeley joined the army and fought in the Anglo Boer War, later becoming a barrister. He helped pay for the Howth Gun Running, when the Irish Volunteers imported £1,500 worth of arms. He assisted in the drilling of national-ist rebels in Belfast before enlisting to fight in the First World War. He was part of the Claims Commission in France and Italy which helped set the amount of reparations the Germans had to pay.

Berkeley's views on Irish politics evolved and he helped found the Irish Dominion League in 1920, which promoted dominion Home Rule. He wrote several books of history and politics, and a volume of schooldays autobiography, before his death in 1955, aged eighty-five.

Andre Cornelius Botha

LHB, RAM; Clontarf, North County, Griqualand West, Ireland (2001-)

Born: 12 September 1975, Johannesburg

Batting

Mts	Inns	NOs	Runs
55	58	1	1,702
Avg	50s	100s	Cts
29.86	11	1	17

Bowling

O	M	R	W
462.3	61	1,834	78
Avg	5WI	10WM	
23.51	-	-	

Highest score: 139 v Herts, Bishop's Stortford 2003
Best bowling: 4-23 v ECB, Malahide 2003

When Afrikaner Andre Botha first came from Johannesburg to Ireland as an eighteen-year-old, he could hardly speak English and struggled to adjust to life off the pitch. A polite but shy young man, he did most of his talking on the field where he adapted well to Irish conditions, being more used to the hard pitches and fast outfields of the South African Highveld.

He rapidly established himself as one of the most feared overseas professionals in Leinster, initially with Clontarf and then from 2000 with North County. A strong left-handed batsman with a cultured cover drive and fearsome pull shot, he punished anything loose while maintaining a cautious defence, necessary on many Irish pitches with their vagaries of bounce and pace.

In many ways, however, it was with the ball that Botha showed his true worth, being able to combine a nagging length with a consistent off-stump line at a fast-medium pace that was more than many club batsmen could handle.

After a few years avoiding winter by turning out for Clontarf until September and then returning to South Africa to play provincial cricket for Griqualand West, Botha decided to make Ireland his home and he turned his attentions to qualifying for the national side.

He made his inauspicious debut at the end of the 2001 season, having been selected as an overseas player against Wiltshire in the 2002 C&G Trophy qualifying round, where he was out lbw first ball and took 1-50. Two weeks later though, in Southampton, he scored 75 and took 3-30 against Hampshire County Board XI.

By the 2003 season he had qualified as an Irish player and quickly established himself as a mainstay of the middle-order and a front-line bowler. Fellow South African Adrian Birrell had taken over as national coach after the disappointing tenure of former New Zealand captain Ken Rutherford and Botha was a crucial part of the rebuilding process.

He scored 139 against Hertfordshire in Bishop's Stortford in August 2003, his only century for Ireland to date. Having made it past 75 on seven occasions since then, that tally should really be considerably more.

A little hit-and-miss with the bat, he has been accused of being slightly impulsive early on before really establishing himself in the innings and, for his ability, he should really have a higher average than something just below 30. But with the ball he has been Ireland's most dependable performer in recent times and top wicket taker,

mastering the basics very well and mixing up his pace with good effect.

Despite his South African roots, Botha has been a thoroughly committed Irishman over the last few years and his dedication to the cause has never been doubted.

'He is an out-and-out team man and has been one of the cornerstones of our success over the last few years,' says Birrell.

James Chrysostom Boucher
RHB, OB; Civil Service, Phoenix and Ireland (1929-54)

100 GREATS

Born: Dublin, 22 December 1910
Died: Fuengirola, Spain, 25 December 1995

Batting

Mts	Inns	NOs	Runs
60	103	15	1161
Avg	**50s**	**100s**	**Cts**
13.19	3	-	42

Bowling

O	M	R	W
1597.1	371	4684	307
Avg	**5WI**	**10WM**	
15.26	31	7	

Highest innings: 85 v MCC, Rathmines 1936
Best bowling: 7-13 v New Zealand, Rathmines 1937

Just a handful of cricketers produced in Ireland could have played the game at Test level; Jimmy Boucher was one of them. In an career that stretched over a quarter of a century, he played sixty times for Ireland, taking 307 wickets, a record only bettered by Dermott Monteith in the 1980s. His bowling style was unique. His stock ball was a big off-break, delivered from a fifteen-yard jinking run-up at a pace not much short of medium. He was gifted with a hand 'like a bunch of bananas', and bowled with an exaggerated tweak of those extraordinary fingers.

His real magic, however, was in his mastery of accuracy and flight – the late dipping ball deceived hundreds of batsmen, and he picked up most of his wickets from catches at short leg, where he often posted three men. No matter the conditions or circumstances, he would never open the bowling, preferring to wait until the shine was off the ball. He was always an attacking bowler, believing negative play was not part of the game.

He made his senior debut at the age of fourteen for Civil Service, before joining the neighbouring club, Phoenix, in 1927. He was still a red-headed schoolboy at Belvedere College when he was first capped two years later. His club records are unlikely to ever be beaten: in 405 matches he took 1,303 wickets at 11.48 (only two others – barely – passed a thousand), he took five wickets in an innings 124 times, including nine-for twice against Merrion, and five hat-tricks. The statistics are legion; a handful will have to suffice to illustrate his achievements.

In the first four matches of the 1943 season he took 27 for 72 (5-15, 6-7, 7-17, 9-33 including the hat-trick). Strangely, he didn't top the bowling averages that year, but he did do so on ten other occasions.

As a batsman ('the best number eight in the world', he used to say) he was no slouch, scoring 7,545 runs at 20.55 (4 centuries, 31 fifties) in club cricket (topping the provincial averages in 1939), and 1,100 runs for Ireland.

He won eight cup medals, five league medals and five trophies as leading all-rounder.

Boucher topped the English first-class averages in Wisden on three occasions: 1931, 1937 and cricket's epochal summer of 1948. He was first to 200 wickets, and 300 for Ireland, and is the only man to take 100 against Scotland.

Many touring sides fell foul of Boucher, and lived to spread his fame. He won the respect of some of the giants of the age, men such as Herbert Sutcliffe, Wally Hammond, the Nawab of Pataudi and Stan McCabe. For Ireland, one of his finest hours was in 1937 when he ran

through the New Zealanders, taking 7-13 as the tourists collapsed to 64 all out. In 1936 he clean bowled four Indian batsmen in taking 6-30.

In 1947 a strong South African batting side were humbled in a 'fill-in' match arranged when the original fixture ended with an Irish defeat in one day. In his historical work *Cricket in Ireland*, Pat Hone described how the tourists 'had almost as much difficulty in dealing with Boucher's off-breaks as the Irishmen had had with those of (Athol) Rowan the previous day. In a truly fine spell of 18 overs, Boucher had seven of them out for 39 runs.' His Irish teammate Donald Shearer, recalled: 'I was fielding in the middle of three short legs. Dudley Nourse, who was captaining South Africa, had made 5 when he played forward outside his off-stump. The leg stump was knocked over. He looked around in amazement, caught my eye, and simply shrugged his shoulders. He couldn't believe it.'

Opportunities for Irish lads to try out for counties were non-existent in those days, but all knowledgeable observers who saw him bowl say there is no question that he would have had a long and successful county career in England, and would certainly have played Test cricket. Lord Tennyson invited him to go with his side to India in 1937 but did not follow up in writing and Boucher couldn't secure the time off from the ESB.

For almost half a century his influence on cricket in Ireland was immense. He was honorary secretary of the ICU from 1954-73 and acted as a selector of the national team from 1963-76. After his retirement he spent winters in Spain but always returned to Dublin for the cricket season. He liked to travel, especially to France, but his main interests were sporting, being a member of Royal Dublin and a keen supporter of Old Belvedere rugby club. The journalist and broadcaster Henry Kelly was among those who benefited from Boucher's coaching while at Belvedere College. He wrote about those days in an article in the *Sunday Tribune* in 1990: 'One fine evening at our school ground just outside Dublin, Boucher had assembled a squad of aspirant youths, myself included. He had undertaken to coach us until we dropped or got it right. Some were in their late teens; others in their early twenties. At one stage he looked around and enquired where one of our number was. "Oh, sir", came a reply, "it's his stag night this evening. He's getting married on Saturday." Jimmy's eyes widened. He stopped short, silent, amazed. Eventually, he spluttered: "What? In the middle of the cricket season?"'

The game of cricket, to which he gave so much in a long and active life, was everything to Jimmy Boucher.

Jeremy Paul Bray ———————————— 100
LHB, RAO; Phoenix, Clontarf, Eglinton, New South Wales and Ireland (2002-) GREATS

A big, powerful left-handed opening batsman from Australia, Jeremy Bray terrorised league bowlers in Leinster for several years as an overseas professional for the Clontarf and Phoenix clubs before qualifying for his adopted country.

And it took him little time to show what he could do at that level as well. In just his second game for Ireland in 2003, Bray hit 67 not out, sharing an unbeaten stand of 183 for the first wicket with a rampant Jason Molins (107 not out), as Ireland beat Test nation Zimbabwe by ten wickets at Stormont, Belfast.

Since then he has been a crucial member of the Ireland set-up that has beaten quality sides including the West Indies, Gloucestershire and Surrey as well as qualifying for the 2007 ICC World Cup and winning the 2005 ICC Intercontinental Cup.

Indeed it was at that first-class Intercontinental Cup in Namibia that he registered his highest score to date and came within eight runs of Ivan Anderson's all-time Ireland record of 198 not out. Bray's 190 against the United Arab Emirates in Windhoek during the semi-final was a masterclass in concentration and sound technique on a dream batting wicket but in hot, energy-sapping conditions at high altitude. He shared a 304-run partnership for the third wicket with Niall O'Brien, a record stand and the only Irish partnership in history worth more than 300. In the end, Ireland progressed to the final of the competition, where they beat Kenya, with Bray contributing 46 and 64. In total, during the four matches of the 2005 Intercontinental Cup, Bray scored 543 runs at an average of nearly 78.

He learned his cricket in Sydney playing for Petersham and St George cricket clubs and he

Born: 30 November 1973, Sydney, Australia

Batting

Mts	Inns	NOs	Runs
54	59	1	1,859
Avg	50s	100s	Cts
32.05	10	4	29

Highest score: 190 v United Arab Emirates, Windhoek 2005

represented Australia under-19s and New South Wales before making the trip to Ireland. He married an Irish woman he met in Sydney and in 1998 the couple settled down in her native County Kilkenny where Bray works as a fitness instructor. Australia's loss was definitely Ireland's gain and he made his debut in 2002 as a twenty-eight-year-old who had broken many of the Leinster scoring records. As with all the best opening batsmen, Bray is a greedy accumulator of runs and will never throw his wicket away, no matter how many he has scored or how tired he feels.

He came in for criticism for being susceptible to getting out lbw early in his innings as he liked to put his right leg down the pitch and play across the front of it. But, recognising that flaw in his technique, he has tried to cut it out of his game and although he remains a little fragile early in his innings, he works hard at getting established while not forgetting to latch on to anything loose, even from the first ball.

To date he has scored four centuries for Ireland, with only Anderson (seven) having hit more. His first came against Denmark at the end of the 2003 season, when he scored 143 at Malahide in Dublin, he followed this up the following season with 116 against the MCC at Limavady and in 2005 he fired two more, 135 against the Netherlands at Stormont and that memorable 190 against the UAE in Namibia. In addition to his four official hundreds, he has also scored three other centuries in Ireland colours that were not recognised as capped matches.

Bray is one of the fittest members of the Ireland team despite being one of the oldest, and has managed to combine opening the batting with keeping wicket in one-day matches as the need arose. With first-choice keeper O'Brien often on duty with his County Kent, Bray stood in with reasonable success for competitions such as the 2006 C&G Trophy and other matches. He has even bowled in seven Ireland matches, a brand of accurate off-spin that has proved quite successful at club level. And although he is yet to take his first international wicket, he has an enviable economy rate of less than 2. But it is for his batting that he will be judged, and his career average of around 32 for Ireland certainly puts him near the top of Irish opening batsmen. That said, it is not likely to be an average that will have him resting on his laurels, as he knows for the talent he possesses and application he demonstrates, it could and should be higher. A high number of one-day games, often played on pitches that are slower, lower and with more lateral movement than is ideal for free-scoring batting, means that anything above 30 is considered excellent for Irish players. Bray's first-class average of almost 50 is possibly a better gauge.

National coach Adrian Birrell says he feels Bray still has some of his best performances ahead of him. 'He is the outstanding batsman in the team,' said Birrell. 'His career average is less than it should be. I think if he continues to play as long as he can, he will end up averaging mid-40s. He is going to have a very good season at some stage,' he said.

Bray is a popular and respected member of the team and although perhaps not really captain material, he has amassed plenty of experience and knowledge from playing cricket at a high level and is not afraid to offer advice or guidance where it is needed.

'He is a very dedicated guy who works very hard on his fitness and his batting,' said Birrell. 'He has a hunger for runs like no one else in Irish cricket and I think his league performances show that. He is a great team man, always very vocal in the dressing room and he has a good sense of humour.'

Francis Henry Browning

RHB, WK; Dublin University, Civil Service, Phoenix and Ireland (1888-1909)

Born: 23 June 1868, Kingstown, Dublin
Died: 26 April 1916, Dublin

Batting

Mts	Inns	NOs	Runs	
39	64	2	1322	
Avg	**50s**	**100s**	**Cts**	**Sts**
21.62	7	-	33	23

Bowling: 3-0-15-0
Highest innings: 94 v Combined Services, Portsmouth, 1893

Frank Browning was a tough little opening batsman whose Ireland career spanned twenty-one years, a period in which he played many a vital innings for the side. He seemed to save his finest performances for the best opponents, principally the touring sides. His greatest hour was probably for a Trinity past and present XI against the 1905 Australians when he made a fifty in each innings against 'Tibby' Cotter, the fastest bowler in the world at the time.

A cousin of the Hones, he was educated in England at Marlborough College, and entered Trinity in October 1886. He was picked for Ireland two years later without any great weight of runs behind him, but impressed with 39 against I Zingari on his second appearance In 1889 he racked up 869 runs (including two centuries) for Trinity and a reputed 2,000 in all games. His highest score for the club came in 1891 when he made 150 against Leinster.

WG Grace brought a United South of England XI to Trinity in 1890, and Browning showed great character in compiling a 50, which he followed with 68 against a strong Cambridge side.

Both Trinity and Ireland toured England in 1893, and Browning was in rich form on both adventures. Against Warwickshire for Trinity he made 84 and took two stumpings to set up a 203 runs win, while he made 32 and 73 against Essex, who included Charles Kortright, reputedly the fastest bowler the game has ever seen. In August he made his Ireland best 94 against the Combined Services, following with 41 at the Oval against Surrey.

He was a compact man, and an unfussy player who favoured punchy drives. On Sir Timothy O'Brien's 1902 tour of England, he made 49 against London County, 56 against Oxford and 44 against Cambridge. He was consistency personified, racking up 15 consecutive double figure innings between 1902 and 1907. He was the first to make 1,000 runs for Ireland and captained his country fourteen times. His last appearances for Ireland were on the 1909 tour to North America when his batting let him down.

Browning held a unique double in being president of both the cricket and rugby unions. In the latter role he helped form a 'pals' regi- ment of rugby men who fought in the First World War. Browning himself was commanding officer of an unarmed home guard-style unit who were fired upon by rebels on the first day of the Easter Rising in 1916. Browning was mortally wounded and died shortly afterwards in Beggar's Bush barracks.

Rev. J Byrne
RHB, RARM; Dublin University, Vice-Regal and Ireland (1873-76)

100 G R E A T S

Born: unknown
Died: unknown

Batting

Mts	Inns	NOs	Runs
3	6	0	68
Avg	100s	50s	Cts
11.33	-	-	1

Bowling

O	M	R	W
211.1	97	269	27
Avg	5WI	10WM	
9.9	3	1	

Highest score: 35 v I Zingari, Vice-Regal, 1876
Best bowling: 9-37 v I Zingari, Phoenix CC, 1873

The Rev. Byrne was a round-arm bowler who played three games for Ireland, all against I Zingari. His debut in September 1873 – a 12-a-side game – was a sensation, with Byrne taking 9-48 and 9-37, a match return of 77.1-42-85-18. IZ were set 108 to win but Byrne's performance meant they fell 12 short.

He missed the next visit of I Zingari, but he was back in 1875 for an 11-a-side fixture. First time around he took 2-40, but in the second innings he was unplayable, returning magnificent figures of 25-19-10-5 as Ireland won by 201 runs.

His final cap was also at the Vice-Regal Grounds. In the first innings he bowled 57 four ball overs, taking 1-89, following it with 1-45. While he was not successful at his primary task, he was a revelation with the bat. In the first innings he made 16, the second highest score, and with Walshe of Phoenix took the score from 74-9 to 101 all out. In the second innings he made a career best 35, adding 85 for the ninth wicket with Frank Kempster, who scored the first century for Ireland.

Byrne had better luck for the Vice-Regal against IZ in the same week, taking 14 wickets as the Lord Lieutenant's club won by an innings. The great scholar and wit JP Mahaffy was on the Vice-Regal side and quoted Aristotle – 'it is the simplest things that we find the most unintel-ligible' – to describe Byrne's bowling.

He was educated at Santry School and Trinity, which he entered in November 1869. He played on the second XI in 1871, before winning his colours on the first XI in the following two seasons.

In 1872 he averaged a reasonable 13 with the bat, while his bowling analysis of 293.3-118-245-33 (7.4) was second best for the club. He was second in the averages again in 1873, with 180-85-235-24 for an average of 9.7. He won a presentation bat from the club for an unrecorded feat – though likely to have been a hat-trick – against Phoenix. He also played rugby for the university, twice winning colours.

He graduated in 1873, and is likely to have been ordained that year as the prefix Rev. begins to appear in scorecards. He was recruited to serve as chaplain in the Vice-Regal Lodge, a move likely to have been motivated by his crick-eting skills (c/f GF Barry). Little else is known about Byrne's life – even his name seems to have evaded historians. It may have been Joseph, as the only clergyman called Byrne who was active in the early 1880s had that name. That Byrne was Dean of Clonfert and had his parish in Omagh, County Tyrone.

100 GREATS

Mark Francis Cohen
RHB; Carlisle and Ireland (1980-94)

A member of the Carlisle club in Dublin, which has since disbanded, Cohen was a talented and meticulous opening batsman who attracted the attentions of the English counties at a time when they didn't usually cast their nets further west than Glamorgan. One of two members of the tiny Dublin Jewish com-munity on this list, Cohen was a club-mate of the other, Jason Molins, who is also an opening batsman.

A prodigious talent as a schoolboy, Cohen enjoyed phenomenal success at underage level, including six successive centuries, making his senior club debut at just fourteen and later scoring 371 runs at an average of 93 in the 1979 Under-19 Esso Cup competition. He made his full international debut the following year, scoring 43 against Wales at Rathmines, but his excellent technique and solid defence had

already caught the attentions of the Middlesex scouts. He was on the books at Lord's and later Sophia Gardens but was not able to establish a place for himself at that level. He returned to the Ireland team at the very end of the 1982 season, scoring 59 not out against Warwickshire, again at Rathmines (in fact, four of Cohen's first five caps were won at that south Dublin venue).

But an inability to score runs quickly and a tendency not to adapt to changing circum-stances of individual matches meant he was not always a favourite with Irish selectors and he was in and out of the team during the following two or three years. In his early years he was accused of being a selfish player but he gradually devel-oped a niche as someone who could anchor the innings as those around him would adopt a more aggressive approach. On a tough tour to Zimbabwe in 1986, Cohen scored three half-

Mark Francis Cohen
continued

Born: 27 March 1961, Cork

Batting

Mts	Inns	NOs	Runs
69	96	8	2,519
Avg	50s	100s	Cts
28.62	17	2	29

Highest score: 118 v Sussex, Malahide 1987

centuries against good bowling and thus finally convinced the selectors that he was worthy of a regular place in the side.

He went on to win sixty-nine caps for Ireland, hitting 17 fifties and 2 centuries in a total of 96 innings, not a bad ratio of one success for every five knocks. He was a reliable and consistent presence for seven or eight years and managed to adapt his game, improving his strike-rate somewhat in the process.

Both his hundreds came against county opposition. He made 118 and 45 against Sussex at Malahide in 1987 and two years later, scored an unbeaten 100 at Bristol against Gloucestershire as bowlers of the quality of England internationals David Lawrence and Mark Alleyne failed to get through his dour defence.

Cohen retired from representative cricket on a personal high after the ICC Trophy in Kenya, scoring a solid 74 against Canada and continued to play for Carlisle in the Leinster leagues. He became a figure on the international social scene for a time when his then girlfriend, Diana Hayden, won the 1997 Miss World competition.

Osmund David Colhoun
WK, RHB; Sion Mills, RUC and Ireland (1959-1979)

Born: 6 June 1938, Sion Mills

Batting

Mts	Inns	NOs	Runs	
87	89	46	296	
Avg	**50s**	**100s**	**Cts**	**Sts**
6.88	-	-	148	42

Highest score: 36 v MCC, Rathmines 1974

Ireland's joint most-capped wicketkeeper to date, with eighty-seven appearances, Ossie Colhoun was an automatic choice behind the stumps for twenty years between 1959 and 1979. With a quick eye and even quicker hands, Colhoun was able to stand up to all but the very quickest bowlers around at that time, including the far-from-pedestrian Roy Torrens and Dougie Goodwin.

Colhoun's game behind the stumps was all about pressure. Standing up made sure batsmen stayed in their crease while it also gave him the opportunity to have a little word in the striker's ear if the need arose.

'He was a fearsome presence behind the stumps, always full of wise cracks and talking people off their game,' said 2005 Irish Cricket Union chairman and former Strabane player Joe Doherty. 'He was into the whole thing of winding opponents up and playing mind games with them before it was the done thing.'

Most of the time off the pitch, Colhoun was quite a shy, reserved character but once he took to the field he was transformed into a bubbly, outgoing personality. A drummer at one time with the well-known showband, 'Clipper Carlton', he carried his on-stage personality on to the cricket field. Not unlike his boyhood hero, former England Test keeper Godfrey Evans, Colhoun had a great ability to lift the team when spirits were low.

Standing up to the stumps Colhoun's lightning hands also gave him another advantage. 'He had a great talent where he could have dropped two catches in one over and no one in the ground would have known except maybe the batsman. He had a great way of tossing the ball up as if to say: 'No he didn't hit that,'' recalled Torrens.

That said, he didn't drop many catches and he continues to hold most of the records for Irish glovemen. In a total of eighty-seven matches he took 191 dismissals including 148 catches and 42 stumpings. In comparison, Ireland's other great wicketkeeper, Paul Jackson, also won eighty-seven caps and captured 132 dismissals (103 catches, 29 stumpings) although he played more one-day games than Colhoun.

A genuine number 11 batsman, Colhoun was very limited with the bat. He had a solid defence and often played the role of night–watchman with good success but never threatened to score heavily, as shown by his batting statistics. He had a top score of 36 against the MCC at Lord's but his overall average was less than seven and he is second in the all–time list of ducks with 17 (one fewer than Jimmy Boucher).

During a game against Scotland at Greenock in 1972, Ireland were staring defeat in the face but Colhoun was there and stonewalling an increasingly frustrated Scottish attack. About fifteen minutes from the close, with nine wickets having fallen and the fielders crowding around him, Colhoun appeared to be hit on the fingers and immediately threw down the bat and tore off his glove with agony all over his face. No one doubted that he was in genuine pain when they saw how contorted one of his fingers was. Doctors were called, the finger was prodded and poked and eventually, after a break of some time, Colhoun manfully resumed. Of course, it had been an old injury but as good as his defence was, he knew they couldn't get him out when the bowlers weren't bowling. He made nine runs in ninety minutes at the crease that afternoon and the match was saved.

Colhoun was a natural athlete and apart from being an energetic wicketkeeper, he also played in goal for the Royal Ulster Constabulary football team for several years. He was a sporting all–rounder and arguably the best to pull on the keeping gloves for Ireland.

Andrew Daniel Comyn

RHB/LB/WK; Dublin University, Phoenix, Co. Galway and Ireland (1893-1904)

Dan Comyn, a tigerish opening bat of the Golden Age, still holds the record score for Ireland in Ireland. The 157 he rattled up against I Zingari at Phoenix in 1897 was hailed as 'brilliance seldom seen on this ground'. With Ireland in some difficulty, he added 201 for the sixth wicket with Drummond Hamilton – the only double century stand for Ireland until 1976 – and having passed his century in 160 minutes he hit out. *The Freeman's Journal* gushed that 'Anything like his hitting has not been seen for a very long time. Never have we seen the County Galway man play better'.

Born in the east Galway town of Kilconnell, Comyn was the second of three brothers – all cricketers – and great grandson of 'the Liberator', Daniel O'Connell. He attended Clongowes Wood in Co. Kildare, the strongest cricketing school in the land at the time. Pat Hone averred that 'An eleven of Old Clongownians at the end of the last century would have been good enough to challenge any Irish eleven on equal terms', and certainly John Hynes, Bill Harrington, Jack Meldon and Tom Ross (who all feature in this book) were giants of the era.

He entered Trinity in 1891, and again he was part of a powerful side. The university played at least one game each year against a county or touring team and Comyn enjoyed the challenge more than anyone. In thirteen such three-day games he made 600 runs, including 3 fifties and 117 v Leicestershire when the college won by an innings and 136 runs. He also made 76 against WG Grace's Gloucestershire in 1894, and the great doctor became a good friend of the red-headed student, later travelling to Galway for shooting expeditions. The following year Trinity played four first-class games, and Comyn did well in these games and made four centuries in other games.

A short, rotund, sturdy batsman, Comyn was first capped in 1893, going in at No.6 against the United Services at Portsmouth and making 51 in adding 114 for the sixth wicket with John Hynes. One of his finest innings for Ireland was

Born: 23 September 1872, Ballinderry, Kilconnell, County Galway
Died: 23 May 1949, Dublin

Batting

Mts	Inns	NOs	Runs	
16	25	0	734	
Avg	**50s**	**100s**	**Cts**	**Sts**
29.36	3	1	6	1

Bowling

O	M	R	W	Avg
9	2	34	0	-

Highest innings: 157 v I Zingari, Phoenix Park, 1896

one of just 39 against MCC at Lord's in 1902, when Ireland were all out for 106. Facing top-class bowling in Albert Trott and JW Hearne, *Wisden* reported that 'only Comyn showed any real ability to cope'.

Comyn finished his Ireland career in 1904, but continued to play for Galway until the outbreak of the Great War. His nephews, Noel and Acheson Kelly, played for Ireland and Trinity in the 1920s.

100 GREATS — Gordon Cooke

RHB, RAM; Berryburn, Cumber Claudy, Eglinton, Ardmore, Limavady and Brigade
Ireland (1994-2005)

A right-arm seam bowler who could generate good pace in the right conditions, Gordon Cooke made his debut for Ireland while still only eighteen years of age. By the time he retired (the first time) he had just turned twenty-five but had already won fifty-six international caps. Very highly rated in his native North-West, he played for several clubs during his career including Ardmore, Eglinton, Limavady and Brigade.

A fluent run-up and uncomplicated delivery, Cooke had an economical action and was known for his ability to make batsmen struggle for time while giving nothing away in line and length. He was clearly a hugely talented cricketer and apart from his

bowling, he was also a much under-rated, free-scoring, lower-order batsman and brilliant fielder.

Following an uninspiring start to his international career where he only took more than one wicket in a match once during his first eight games, Cooke was left out of the Irish team for much of 1995 and the entire 1996 season. He was recalled in 1997 and following a number of good performances, particularly against Glamorgan and the MCC in 1998, he became a regular name in the starting eleven. He took 4-60 against the touring South Africans at Downpatrick later that summer and also took three wickets in an innings twice against Scotland in the same season.

33

Gordon Cooke
continued

Born: 24 July 1975, Derry

Batting

Mts	Inns	NOs	Runs
66	48	18	481
Avg	50s	100s	Cts
16.03	-	-	15

Bowling

O	M	R	W
615.2	76	2,771	84
Avg	5WI	10WM	
32.99	1	-	

Highest score: 38 not out v Denmark, The Hague 1998
Best bowling: 5-55 v Bangladesh, Limavady 2004

But he didn't really set the world on fire and did not always make himself available for selection or Ireland training sessions. Cooke decided to give up representative cricket in 2000 and, still only in his mid-twenties, he returned to league cricket and continued to dominate at that level as the spearhead of the bowling attack for his club.

He was eventually coaxed out of retirement in 2004 and was recalled for a one-day match against the West Indies at Stormont in July of that year.

He performed significantly better after he made his comeback and seemed to respond well to the professional approach taken by national coach Adrian Birrell. In the ten matches he played in 2004 and 2005 (all of which were one-dayers), he took a very respectable 19 wickets at an average of just over 20 and although he didn't bat much, he averaged 26.50 when he did get

the opportunity to flash the blade during that period. Although he took three wickets in the final of the 2005 ICC Trophy against Scotland at Castle Avenue, Dublin, Cooke was criticised for bowling erratically in an expensive spell that cost 70 runs in nine overs. He was dropped for the ICC Intercontinental Cup campaign later that season and very quickly disappeared from the international scene.

'He was nearer to being a genuine all-rounder than he is often given credit for, even at club level,' said 2005 chairman of the Irish Cricket Union Joe Doherty. 'I think he probably batted too deep even in North-West cricket… He became known for not being available for matches but he must have been available for plenty because in the end he played sixty-six times.

'Certainly, he wasn't someone who could waltz away from work whenever he felt like it but he did his bit for Ireland, that's for sure.'

Simon Charles Corlett

RHB, RAF; Oxford University, CIYMS, North of Ireland and Ireland (1974-87)

Born: 18 January 1950, Blantyre, Nyasaland (now Malawi)

Batting

Mts	Inns	NOs	Runs
73	80	19	1,045
Avg	50s	100s	Cts
17.13	4	-	48

Bowling

O	M	R	W
1882.2	438	5,387	233
Avg	5WI	10WM	
23.12	8	-	

Highest score: 60 v Scotland, Castle Avenue 1977
Best bowling: 7-44 v Surrey, Rathmines 1978

Born and raised in the east African country of Nyasaland, Corlett moved to England as a young man and soon made an impression as a spin bowler for Worksop College in Nottinghamshire and then Oxford University. He played a few games for Nottinghamshire 2nds while still a schoolboy in 1967 and when he went up to Oxford he was awarded his blue in 1971 and 1972. He toured the Far East with a combined Oxford/Cambridge team in '72 and late that summer he moved full-time to Belfast where his father had been working for Gallaher's tobacco firm since 1964.

Irish cricket would be forever grateful that he chose here to make his home and he quickly made a big impression. For the end of the 1972 season and all of 1973, he played for junior club CIYMS but it was clear from an early stage that his future did not lie in the lower reaches of domestic cricket and that in order to break into representative Irish cricket, he would have to change clubs.

An elegant and technically correct bowler of considerable pace and accuracy (he had changed from spinner to opener), Corlett was much too good for his CIYMS teammates and in 1974 he moved to the Ormeau Road and North of Ireland, traditionally one of the strongest clubs in Ulster. Later that same year, Corlett received a letter from then honorary secretary of the ICU Derek Scott informing him of his selection for Ireland and asking him to send a cheque for £50 to cover travel expenses to the Netherlands. On his debut, he took 2-33 and

4–88 against the Dutch at Amstelveen and so began a long and successful career lasting 13 years and 73 matches.

In that time he took 233 wickets (the third highest) at an average of 23.12 and an economy rate of less than 3, making him one of the best bowlers Ireland has ever had. He had a high action that enabled him to get extra bounce and he often seemed to bowl within himself. His smooth run-up and fluid action meant his body was never put under too much undue strain, allowing him to continue bowling long spells without a break and his ability to swing the ball both ways was often too much for all but the best batsmen to handle.

After that impressive debut in Holland, Corlett soon became an automatic choice. He took five wickets in matches against the MCC and Wales later that summer and the following year took 7–69 against Denmark at Ringsted. On eight occasions he took five wickets or more in an innings for Ireland, his best coming in a drawn match against Surrey at Rathmines when he bowled 22.3 overs and took 7–44. In interprovincials he took 201 wickets at 12.29 each.

'Simon was the number one opening bowler of my time, even better than (Alec) O'Riordan,' said former teammate John Elder. 'Pace, grace, technical ability – he had it all. Corlett and (Dermott) Monteith in the same team gave it two exceptional all-rounders,' he said.

Although primarily a bowler, Corlett was a more-than-capable batsman and he scored four half-centuries for Ireland. He was also a fine gully fielder, taking 48 catches, putting him third in the all-time list for non-wicketkeepers. His highest score with the bat was 60 and came against Scotland at Castle Avenue in 1977 when he was batting at a slightly elevated sixth in the order.

He holds the Irish record for an eighth-wicket stand of 150 with Junior McBrine that they set against Scotland at Coleraine in 1987 and his other 2 fifties came against Scotland (again) in 1976 and Wales in 1981. Indeed, although not strictly a batsman he is one of only forty-one players (out of more than 600 capped players) to get past the 1,000-run mark for Ireland, giving him good cause for the title of all-rounder.

Having come over from Nyasaland via England, Corlett quickly became one of the most feared and respected bowlers on the domestic club scene. In 1982, he took 104 wickets for North, the first player known to break the 100 mark in competitions. The previous year he had set another record, taking all ten wickets in a senior game against Downpatrick.

Having opened the bowling as a seamer, he would often come back later in the innings as a very accomplished off-spinner, capable of turning the ball on even a docile pitch and he was even able to bowl left-arm if the need ever arose.

Known as 'the Growler' for the aggressive way he stared at batsmen, Corlett was one who took his cricket very seriously and always tried to get the best out of himself. He kept fit in winter by playing hockey and no matter how long the spell of bowling he was always ready to give more. He retired from representative cricket at the end of the 1987 season when he was still capable of putting in top-class performances and it was called 'a major body blow to Irish cricket' by one commentator, Clarence Hiles, who was writing in the 1988 Ireland season programme. 'We can ill afford to lose a player of such quality… Simon leaves behind a marvellous chronicle of outstanding performances against the cream of world cricket. He was simply in that class. We may not see the likes of him for many years to come, such was his brilliance,' wrote Hiles.

After retirement, Corlett served as a selector both for Ireland and the NCU. He was the first president of Belfast Harlequins, the club formed through the merger of North and Collegians rugby in 2001 and in 2003, he was made president of the ICU. In 2005, North cricket moved to the Civil Service club at Stormont and he became president there too.

'There is no doubt that he would be in a lot of people's all-time eleven,' said 121-capped all-rounder Alan Lewis. 'He had an in-swinger, an out-swinger, he could bowl off-spin beautifully, was a good lower-order batsman, brilliant fielder and a fantastic competitor. On the field, he had it all and is surely one of the all-time best,' said Lewis.

RHB; Dublin University, Cork County, Phoenix and Ireland (1884-88)

Born: Monkstown, Cork, 23 September 1863
Died: Cork, 28 December 1948

Batting

Mts	Inns	NOs	Runs
11	16	-	242
Avg	50s	100s	Cts
15.12	-	-	6

Highest innings: 45 v Canada, Rathmines 1887

Dominic Cronin was a Corkman who learned the game at the hands of the Jesuits in Beaumont College, Old Windsor near London. He was a natural, and was in the school XIs for football and cricket for three years, captaining at cricket in 1880 and 1881 when he was singled out as a 'reliable run-getter'. He entered Trinity College Dublin in January 1882 to study law but as he wasn't in residence he wasn't eligible to play for the club and instead turned out – 'with some success' – for Cork County. An abscess to his right hand further delayed his debut for the university but he won his place on the Trinity first XI towards the end of the 1883 season and never left the side for five seasons.

In 1884, when he topped the averages with 285 runs at 28.5, he made 50 and 102 against North of Ireland and won his first two caps for Ireland. In 1886 he made centuries for Trinity against the Curragh Brigade and the Dublin Garrison, the latter a blistering 165 not out in

just 27 overs. He finished that season with 509 runs at 36.5.

The following year he made another brisk century in 19 overs against Leinster at Rathmines, which he followed with 117 against County Meath, giving him 531 runs for the season at 37.9. He made 95 for the Trinity past & present selection against the All England XI in 1887.

On graduation he joined the well-worn path from College Park to Phoenix and made 67 against his former teammates. Later that summer of '88 he made 122 for the Vice-Regal XI against Co. Meath.

In Cork he was fortunate to bat in tandem with the great John Dunn as the Tasmanian made 201 in an afternoon against Leinster in 1884, with Cronin making fifty. Dunn and Cronin set a Cork County record of 144 for the 3rd wicket against Na Shuler the same week, with Cronin contributing 39 and Dunn 197. He wasn't much of a bowler – he was given the ball in another game when Leinster needed one to win in the second innings, and almost hit the square leg umpire. He was, however, a useful racquets player and was Trinity champion on two occasions.

He travelled to America in September 1888 with a side assembled by his fellow student John Hynes and whose thirteen comprised of ten current or recent Trinity men. In a ballot held on the *City of Rome* on the journey across the Atlantic, Cronin was elected captain ahead of Hynes. They had an extensive programme of eight games in Canada and six in the US. Cronin did not excel on the trip, although he made a well-received 37 against Ottawa and an important 48 against Philadelphia. The tour was watched by huge crowds – 10,000 in the final game which Ireland lost with just three minutes left to play. The demands of his legal career meant Cronin rarely played at a high level thereafter.

100 GREATS

John Desmond Curry
LHB, RAO; Donemana, Limavady and Ireland (1992-2001)

Born: 20 December 1966, Strabane

Batting

Mts	Inns	NOs	Runs
50	50	6	1,193
Avg	50s	100s	Cts
27.11	9	1	18

Bowling

O	M	R	W
235.5	17	992	33
Avg	5WI	10WI	
30.06	-	-	

Highest score: 100 v Earl of Arundel's XI, Arundel Castle 2001
Best bowling: 3-28 v USA, Kuala Lumpur 1997

One of the most controversial and enigmatic figures in Irish cricket, Decker Curry was also clearly one of its most talented. As a hard-hitting left-handed batsman, Curry has dominated league cricket for two clubs in his native North-West over the last twenty years or so. He has compiled in the region of 70 senior centuries at that level, one of the most prolific batsman in the history of the domestic game on this island. Strong forearms, built up from his work at an abattoir, together with perhaps the keenest eye and sweetest timing in the country, meant there was nowhere to hide for bowlers who strayed in line or length.

In 1998 he hit 260 not out for Limavady against Dublin side CYM in a 50-over Irish Senior Cup match at Terenure. The adjoining tennis club had to be evacuated as Curry sent a shower of balls in every direction out of the ground. Although it was a one-day match Limavady eventually declared with two overs to go because CYM had run out of balls. In 2003 he made 205 out of a total of 334 for 5 as Limavady beat his former club Donemana in the semi-final of the North-West Cup. His innings lasted just 126 balls and included 22 fours and 10 sixes. Not surprisingly he won the man of the match award that day (he also took three wickets and two catches). In total he has scored four double hundreds, all in one-day games, and one of them – 230 for Donemana against Bready – was in a 40-over match.

For several reasons this level of performance was never really translated to the international arena although he did show glimpses of his genius at crucial times for Ireland.

Primarily an opening batsman, Curry won the man of the match award for his run-a-ball innings of 75 that set up a match-winning total for Ireland against Middlesex in the B&H Cup at Castle Avenue in 1997. It was the first time Ireland had beaten a county in a competitive match and it won him many accolades from his teammates and opponents alike.

Former England Test bowler Angus Fraser, who was playing for Middlesex that day, had this to say: 'Middlesex weren't much of a sledging side and when we found out that this lad could probably break a sheep's neck with his bare hands, we certainly weren't going to say anything to annoy him. Curry opened the batting and belted 75 in no time at all. Simon Cook was playing his first game for Middlesex. He went for 71 off nine overs.'

But Curry was not an easy character for the Irish coaches or selectors to deal with. He did not always make himself available for certain matches and his attendance record at national team training sessions was inconsistent, to say the least. His dedication to Ireland's cause over and above that of his club was often called into question and he had a strong-willed personality, not afraid to tell people what he thought.

It came to a head in Toronto during the disastrous ICC Trophy in 2001, the qualifying tournament for the 2003 ICC Cricket World Cup. After opening the batting and hitting an unbeaten 95 out of a run chase of just 149 against Papua New Guinea, Curry reasonably expected to fulfil the same role in the line-up the next day against Scotland.

Coach Ken Rutherford disagreed, however, and Curry was forced to bat at five. In the end, Curry lasted just six balls and during the break between innings had a very public altercation with Rutherford. Curry and ICU officials agreed that it would be for the best if he returned home immediately. In the event, Ireland lost that game, did not qualify for the World Cup, Rutherford resigned at the end of the season and Curry never played for Ireland again.

His statistics in North-West cricket remain Bradman-esque with no one coming close to the number of centuries that he scored or to his batting average over the last two decades or so. In fifty matches for Ireland he averaged 27.11 with the bat including just one century (against the Earl of Arundel's XI in June 2001) and while these stats are relatively respectable compared to many of his contemporaries, they don't quite match up to the promise that he had and the form that he showed playing week-in, week-out for Donemana or Limavady.

He has also been a very successful slow bowler and one of the best slip fielders in the country. He took 33 wickets at just over 30 for Ireland, held 18 catches and captained the side once during his international career. But such has been his domination of cricket in the North-West that it is likely he will forever be mentioned in those terms rather than what he ever did in the Irish colours.

Peter Joseph Davy
RHB; Pembroke and Ireland (1995-2002)

Born: I July 1974, Dublin

Batting

Mts	Inns	NOs	Runs
44	45	2	1,000
Avg	50s	100s	Cts
23.26	4	2	8

Highest score: 132 v MCC, Lord's 1999

Peter Davy made his Ireland debut as a twenty-one-year-old against Scotland at Castle Avenue, failed to score and promptly disappeared from the international radar for two years. He came back into the side in 1997 for two games, scored 38 in three innings and promptly disappeared again for another two years.

When he was finally given a protracted opportunity in the national team it took him a while to adapt but towards the end of the 1999 season he scored 97 as Ireland beat a South African Academy team that included Justin Ontong, Tyron Henderson and James Bryant by five wickets and then in his very next innings he made 132 against the MCC at Lord's. He smashed 8 sixes in that knock which remains a record for the highest number of maximums in one innings for Ireland.

On his day, Davy was impossible to bowl to. Never afraid to play his shots, he could score quickly and to all parts of the ground. Although a quiet, introverted character off the field, Davy had enormous confidence in his own ability and backed himself to be able to hit any bowler out of the attack regardless of the state of the wicket. At domestic level for his club Pembroke, other teams knew that they needed to get Davy

out early or he could take the game away from them very quickly.

In a way, that strength was also his weakness because he seemed unable or unwilling to adapt his game to suit the situation. He was convinced that he could dominate any bowler in any playing conditions and while that was often true in the Leinster leagues, he was often accused of giving his wicket away playing extravagant shots at inopportune times. And when he played for Ireland those times came more frequently.

As his career developed, the biggest improvement he made was learning how to stay in and he put together some strong periods, batting in the middle order for Ireland. He averaged over 40 in the 2001 ICC Trophy in Toronto, including 104 not out against Canada in Ross Lord Park, in a disappointing tournament for Ireland overall. In total he made exactly 1,000 runs for Ireland at an average of 23.

Davy's identical twin brother John, who since emigrated to London, played twenty-six times for Ireland as a left-arm seam bowler. They were one of three sets of twins to play men's cricket for Ireland, the others being James and Junior McBrine of Donemana CC and the Waughs, Mark and Steve, who both made separate guest appearances under a development initiative instigated by Ali Bacher and funded by Independent Newspapers.

Perhaps as a result of John specialising in bowling and Peter in batting, John was never really given full credit for what he could do with the bat nor Peter with the ball.

'John always did a lot more with the ball but Peter bowled straight,' said former Pembroke player and current Leinster Cricket Union junior secretary Michael Sharp. 'In the lower grades of cricket when they were coming up, Pete took more wickets than John.' And although he batted way down the order for Ireland, John was a useful hitter, scoring an unbeaten half-century in a 100-run tenth-wicket stand with Paul McCrum against Scotland in 1997. It remains a record partnership for the tenth wicket.

'Their application was tremendous when they were kids,' said Sharp. 'They used to come to training as a pair and because one was essentially a bowler and the other essentially a batsman, they used to practice together for hours and hours.'

Thomas Hartigan Dixon
RHB, RFM; Phoenix, Dublin University and Ireland (1927-32)

100
GREATS

In the same way as we gave them Tom Horan and the ancestors of Glenn McGrath and Simon O'Donnell, Irish cricket has always been receptive to having the compliment returned by Australia. From John Dunn in the 1880s up to Trent Johnston and Jeremy Bray in the twenty-first century, Australians have found a warm welcome in Irish cricket sides.

That was certainly the case with Tom Dixon – and his brother Pat – in the 1920s. The Dixons were seemingly inseparable; both were born in India, were educated in South Australia and entered Trinity College Dublin together in October 1925. In later life they became missionaries and died, two years apart, in the Rift Valley of Kenya in the 1980s.

Big Tom was the better cricketer, his 79 wickets at an average of 16.92 places him in the top ten of those with more than 50 wickets. He was a good enough batsman – of the hard-hitting variety – to make a 50 at Lord's.

The Dixons fetched up in Dublin in time for the 1926 season, but found conditions alien and did not find their feet in that first summer. The visit of Northamptonshire in June thrust Tom to the fore, and his medium-pace out-swing claimed six victims at a cost of 42 runs. In the return match in Northampton he took 4-118,

Born: 22 January 1906, Dhapai, Punjab, India
Died: 12 April 1985, Nakuru, Kenya

Batting

Mts	Inns	NOs	Runs
17	28	4	372
Avg	50s	100s	Cts
15.50	1	-	6

Bowling

O	M	R	W
491.3	136	1339	79
Avg	5WI	10WM	
16.95	4	1	

Highest innings: 52 not out v MCC, Lord's, 1931

two to catches held by future Nobel laureate Samuel Beckett.

He had a spectacular season in 1927, taking 61 wickets at 12.5 as Trinity won the league for the first time, and winning his first cap as a substitute against Scotland in July. His debut could hardly have been more impressive, making 21 and 31* with the bat, and 7-51 and 3-79 with the ball. From then until he left Ireland for good, he was an automatic choice. He only once got the chance to face a major touring team, the 1928 West Indians, and his 7-110 and second innings 19 played a vital role in a famous win.

For Trinity he took 339 wickets in seven seasons, in which he also made more than 2,000 runs, including centuries against Phoenix and Ulster. He is one of only four men (Hoey, Heaslip and C W Mellon were the others) to record 1,000 league runs and 100 wickets. He was runner-up to Eddie Ingram for the all-rounders cup in 1929 and 1931.

He captained the club in 1928 and was appointed Ireland captain for 1931 and 1932, winning all four of the games he took charge of, a unique record. At Lord's in '32 his medium-pace swingers were lethal in the morning dew and he took four wickets in the first half-hour. Later in the game he hit 28 runs off one over, nearly killing Nigel Haig with a six that cleared the stand on the clock side of the pavilion as the Middlesex captain made his way to the tennis courts. MCC were beaten before 11.30 on the second morning.

Dixon returned to India on graduation and continued to play to a high level. He was selected for the Viceroy's XI in a first-class fixture and captained Delhi in its inaugural game in the Ranji Trophy in 1934. He played three games for Delhi, two as captain, but never made more than 16 and only took one wicket.

100 GREATS

Brendan Andrew Donaghey
RHB; Sion Mills, Strabane and Ireland (1962-67)

Long-serving honorary secretary of the Irish Cricket Union Derek Scott said that Donaghey was probably the second best Irish batsman after Waringstown's Ivan Anderson until Ed Joyce came on the scene in the late 1990s. However, Scott says he would not be in his top-one-hundred players as remarkably he only played three times for Ireland. He did, however, score a huge amount of runs in his native North-West for Sion Mills and, later, Strabane.

'In club cricket, his was the wicket that all the teams wanted and he was the man that spectators came to see,' said former Strabane teammate and 2004-5 ICU chairman Joe Doherty. 'When Donaghey got to 30 or 40 he invariably went on to make a really big score and it ended up that both sets of supporters would be applauding him,' said Doherty.

'He would have played more times for Ireland but he had work commitments and also ended up in disputes with the Irish Cricket Union over availability. It is a far cry from today when players are taken care of with their expenses and so on. He didn't always make himself available for that reason. That he only won three caps is hard to believe when you view the talent that he had,' he said.

He made his Ireland debut on 1 August 1962 against Pakistan in College Park when he was out for a duck in the first innings and then made an unbeaten 20 as Ireland drew the match. He played one more game that season, a draw against the MCC at Lord's where he batted a long time for his 32 before being dismissed by Eric Bedser in the first innings and 25 in the second.

There was then a break of five years before his third and final cap, against Worcestershire at Sydney Parade, Dublin. There, in the second innings he scored 37 – his highest score for Ireland – before being bowled by England Test

Brendan Andrew Donaghey
continued

Born: 17 May 1941, Sion Mills

Batting

Mts	Inns	NOs	Runs
3	6	1	122
Avg	**50s**	**100s**	**Cts**
24.40	-	-	-

Highest score: 37 v Worcestershire, Sydney Parade 1967

player Norman Gifford. The match ended in a draw meaning that Donaghey never won or lost a match for Ireland.

He is a controversial inclusion in this list for the simple reason that he only played three times for Ireland and didn't exactly set the world on fire when he did. But he dominated club cricket for Sion Mills and later Strabane in the North-West for many years and clearly had the ability if not the inclination to play at a much higher level. He is arguably the finest batsman the North-West has ever produced and certainly rated up there with recent stars Decker Curry and Stephen Smyth.

'Donaghey was the original wristy player. He was a marvellous, marvellous batsman,' said Doherty. 'He played a lot of his shots off the back foot. He was hooking and pulling the ball in North-West cricket before it was fashionable. He would take on the fastest bowlers off the back foot – he had wonderful footwork.

'He didn't lack talent and he certainly had a great belief in his own ability. From a very young age he was cocky and confident and really believed that he could take on anybody. He had very good hands in the field and stood very successfully particularly at second slip.'

Gerald Andrew Anthony Duffy
RHB, LB; Leinster and Ireland (1953-74)

Born: Dublin, 4 November 1930

Batting

Mts	Inns	NOs	Runs
55	78	16	1123
Avg	50s	100s	Cts
18.11	5	-	39

O	M	R	W
740	258	1577	82
Avg	5WI	10WM	
19.23	2	-	

Highest score: 92 v MCC, Castle Avenue, 1970

Best bowling: 6-29 v Australia, Ormeau, 1961

Gerry Duffy was a brilliant all-rounder for Leinster but he peaked at international level far less often than he probably should have done. A wonderful character, Duffy's eccentricities are celebrated in many anecdotes (including how he practiced bowling in the aisle of the jumbo jet that took the Ireland team to the US in 1973). His unassuming manner belied a brilliant cricket mind and skills developed over many years.

He was a quick learner too – the West Indian great Learie Constantine, who coached at Trinity College Dublin several times, recalled a thirteen-year-old lad at St Mary's College in one of his autobiographies: 'I gave him three lessons, and never before or since have I seen such promise in a batsman after so short a period of tuition… If he continues to improve at anything like this rate, and if he comes into County cricket here, he may very well open for England one day'.

He made his senior debut at the age of seventeen, and was on the Ireland side within five years. He was single-minded in his devotion to practice, as clubmate George Mackay explained: 'Oftentimes you would find Gerry practising all day by himself… many a day he turned out for two matches, yet in the fading light that

evening still had the enthusiasm to put in a stint at the nets'.

Duffy's finest hour with the ball came in September 1961 at Ormeau against Australia. Norman O'Neill was in full flow, but Duffy came on with his 'gentle floaters' and induced him to mishit to cover as the tourists collapsed from 143-3 to 209 all out. He took 6-29 off 13.2 overs – and had two catches dropped off him – but was injured and didn't bowl in the second innings. In the famous 1969 win over the West Indies, Duffy held two cracking catches in the gully, scored 15 not out and took 12-8-12-2 in the less celebrated second innings.

To his 82 wickets for Ireland must be added his 944 scalps for Leinster CC, which came at an average of 13.88 and included 54 five wicket innings. As a batsman he was one of the very few to make 10,000 senior runs, averaging 35.27 and scoring nine centuries (all between 1953-62, three in 1953) and 64 fifties. Duffy scored the only double century in the province between 1938 and 1983, which he made against Phoenix at Rathmines in 1955.

He still lies fourteenth in the LCU all-time batting averages and thirteenth in the bowling, his only rival in both top thirties being Alec

Gerald Andrew Anthony Duffy
continued

O'Riordan (sixteenth and first). Duffy won six medals each in league and cup, including doubles in 1953 and 1981.

He collected all of the major individual trophies for batting (five times between 1961-72), bowling (1976) and all-rounders (three times). He was also delighted to win the second-division bowling award in 1985, aged fifty-four, with 30 wickets at 8.00.

It is astonishing he never made a century in 78 innings for Ireland. The closest he came was against MCC at Clontarf in 1970, when he set a new highest score of 79, which he beat in the second innings. At lunch on the third day he was 92*, but was dismissed off the first ball afterwards, 'probably the only delivery in the entire match which did anything untoward'.

Journalist Peter O'Reilly reported how his club Old Belvedere's dressing room resounded with laughter in 1990 when they heard Duffy had been recalled – aged fifty-nine – to play one more senior fixture, his first for several years. The laugh was on the Belvo boys, however, as the man playing in his sixth decade in the top division bowled 20 overs unchanged and took 4-70.

Although he had coached Leinster's u-15s for more than half a century, when he eventually bowed out he was recruited to coach Merrion. There he oversaw an unprecedented run of success and played an important role in the development of the young Joyces. He was a popular winner of the inaugural LCU Hall of Fame award in 2000.

Angus Richard Dunlop
RHB, RAO; YMCA and Ireland (1990-2000)

100 GREATS

One of Ireland's most-capped internationals, Angus Dunlop was a player who improved immeasurably as he progressed through his career. A right-handed batsman of enormous talent, the young Dunlop was often accused of throwing his wicket away playing loose shots and failing to adapt his game to the conditions at hand. When he retired from representative cricket in 2000 at the age of thirty-three he was probably at the peak of his powers. Indeed, in his final match for Ireland (against Scotland) he played what was arguably his finest innings, ending up with 150 in a first-class match at Ayr.

In his 114 caps he scored four centuries – only Ivan Anderson, with seven, has scored more – and he is the only batsman to feature twice in the top ten individual scores for Ireland. A powerfully built man, Dunlop used a mixture of sweet timing and brute force, often appearing to simply lean on the ball before it whistled to the boundary. Particularly strong off his pads, he played the pick-up over square leg to great effect throughout his career.

His international career started very brightly in 1990 when he scored 69 against the MCC at Coleraine but that remained his highest score for the subsequent forty-two matches in Ireland colours when, in 1996, he was out for 99 playing against Wales at Rathmines, Dublin. In the second innings of that game he made 94, becoming the only Irishman to get out for 90-something in each innings, and in his next match he hit 148 runs of real quality against the MCC at Malahide. Former Ireland and YMCA teammate Alan Lewis said it was 'one of the most memorable knocks that I saw in my time'.

By then, Dunlop was a senior member of the team and his batting radically improved as he matured as a player. He took over as captain in 1998 and he blossomed under the more professional approach of Ireland's first full-time national coach Mike Hendrick. Up to that memorable game against Wales, he was averaging just above 18. From that point until the end of his career, his average was over 38. His first-class average for Ireland was an impressive 43.07. One of his finest innings was an unbeaten century he scored

Born: 17 March 1967, Dublin

Batting

Mts	Inns	NOs	Runs
114	128	20	3,164
Avg	50s	100s	Cts
29.30	16	4	40

Bowling

O	M	R	W
354.3	69	1,268	36
Avg	5WI	10WM	
35.22	1	-	

Highest score: 150 v Scotland, Ayr 2000
Best bowling: 5-26 v Wales, Kimmage 1990

against South Africa in Castle Avenue, facing bowlers the likes of Shaun Pollock, Allan Donald and Hansie Cronje, although the attempted reverse sweep he played on 99 was not his finest shot of the day. He is also the only Ireland batsman to score a century at the Ormeau ground in Belfast – and always will be. Three had been dismissed on 99 at the ground before Dunlop beat the hoodoo in 1999 with 112 against Scotland. The ground, which had been the scene of more than 40 internationals, closed in 2001.

Dunlop was a much underused and underrated off-spinner. His best figures of 5-26 came in his very first match but unfortunately he will probably be best remembered for just one over he bowled against the touring Australians in 1993 when a rampant Allan Border hit him for 32, including 5 sixes off the first five balls. The sixth ball of the over was edged for a dou-

ble, keeping both players out of that particular record book. Otherwise Dunlop could have become a latter-day Malcolm Nash, the man Garfield Sobers smashed for six maximums in one over in 1968.

As captain, Dunlop had a good cricketing brain and was not short on confidence in making decisions on the field of play. He could be an intimidating presence for younger players and was not always receptive to suggestions from his less experienced teammates but he could be relied upon to offer a humorous comment or dry witticism in the changing room or on the field of play. He captained Ireland on 40 occasions, with only Jason Molins leading the country in more games. He retired early from representative cricket for work reasons but continues to score runs in Leinster club cricket for YMCA as a feared and respected opponent.

John Dunn

RHB, Surrey, Phoenix, Cork County and Ireland (1887-88)

Born: 8 June 1862, Hobart, Tasmania, Australia
Died: 10 October 1892, Sand Island, Pescadores, Formosa

Batting

Mts	Inns	NOs	Runs
8	11	-	402
Avg	50s	100s	Cts
36.54		2	1

Bowling

O	M	R	W
8	0	36	0
Avg	5WI	10WM	
-	-	-	

Highest score: 126 v All New York, Staten Island 1888

John Dunn represents a group of cricketers whose presence in Ireland was as part of the colonial army that did so much to spread the game in the eighteenth and nineteenth century. It was a Garrison side that played in the first recorded match in 1792 and for the next 130 years most of the major Irish sides relied on military men. Their departure on independence was a serious blow to the game from which it took decades to recover.

In a time when qualifications were not deemed important, several of them played for Ireland, including Frederick Fane of the 61st Regiment in 1865. Ten years later his son, also Frederick, was born at the army camp in the Curragh – and grew up to play fourteen Test matches and captain England.

The finest soldier cricketer was the Australian-born John Dunn, who moved to England aged nine, and was educated at Harrow. He played four times for Surrey in 1881 – when he was an officer cadet at Sandhurst – and a couple of games thereafter for MCC. He joined the Liverpool Regiment in 1882 and was posted to Cork and later Dublin. Lt Dunn made a huge impression on Irish cricket – he made the first double century for Cork County, against Leinster in 1884, the same year he made 197 against Na Shuler. His performances in 1885 were incredible. He batted forty-two times and made 2,264 runs including ten centuries, of which the biggest were 225* v the Civilians of Dublin and 210 against W Hone's XI. The following summer he rattled up six centuries in a week.

Jack Meldon later explained his hunger for runs: 'He used to make a century on the Garrison Ground, then he would get a Tommy to field for him, and bike over to the Phoenix, and bat for PCC, and perhaps have another knock on the Garrison Ground later'.

The Irish Field described him as '5ft 8in in height, dark complexioned, and a perfect model of manly symmetry, with great strength but no lumber'.

He was invited to play for the Gentlemen of Ireland against their Canadian counterparts at Rathmines in 1887, which he marked with innings of 67 and 20. He travelled with the Irish side to North America in the autumn of 1888, finishing the tour with most runs (630) and best average (34), marking the last of his six caps for Ireland with what the *American Cricketer* called an 'attractive and aggressive' 126 v All New York.

On his return to England in 1889 he made 90 for MCC against Glamorgan, earning a call-up for the Gentlemen of England against I Zingari at the Scarborough festival. It was the most exalted company of his cricket career, coming in No.6 behind WG Grace, Charles Thornton,

Drewy Stoddart, Tim O'Brien and Kingsmill Key. He made 1 and 9.

He was promoted to captain and posted to Hong Kong that winter with the Army Service Corps. He continued to score heavily in local and military cricket where he acquired the nickname the 'Grace of the East'. In 1892 he made the first century in the annual fixture between Hong Kong and Shanghai but batted poorly in the return game. A teammate reported that he had been suffering from an astigmatism for some time. On the journey home the P&O ship, the *SS Bokhara,* ran into a typhoon off Taiwan, hit a sandbank and sank. Of the 148 aboard all but 23 were lost, and Dunn, aged thirty, was one of those who died.

100
GREATS

Matthew Damian Dwyer
LHB, LAO; The Hills and Ireland (1998-2001)

Born: 22 February 1959, Dublin

Batting

Mts	Inns	NOs	Runs
51	26	17	60
Avg	50s	100s	Cts
6.67	-	-	17

Bowling

O	M	R	W
163.1	61	1,604	62
Avg	5WI	10WM	
25.87	-	-	

Highest score: 12 not out v Scotland, Malton, Toronto 2001
Best bowling: 4-57 v Australia A, Rathmines 1998

Matt Dwyer, or O'Dwyer as he is more correctly but less frequently known, made his international debut at the ripe old age of thirty-nine having been overlooked for most of his long and very fruitful club career.

A stalwart of The Hills CC in north Dublin, Dwyer was beginning to emerge as a left-arm slow bowler with real talent when the club won senior status in 1982. He went on to win the Leinster provincial bowling award (O'Grady Cup) on five occasions, including four times in five years from 1990-94. But even then and despite most players accepting that he was the best slow bowler in the province of Leinster, Ireland teams continued to be selected without his name being included while other Leinster players got in ahead.

Ironically, by the time he did get his call-up, he was probably a little past his prime but he certainly made the most of his opportunity. Now widely regarded as being the best left-arm slow bowler Ireland has produced since Dermott Monteith, he managed to squeeze in fifty-one matches from his debut against Glamorgan in the 1998 B&H Cup to his final cap three years later, a rain-ruined game against the Australians in Ormeau, Belfast.

From his very first game he showed selectors what they had been missing by taking an impressive 2-40 off ten overs against a Glamorgan side that included Matthew Maynard, Adrian Dale and Robert Croft. Later that season at Rathmines he took 4-57 against a very strong Australia A side managed by Allan Border, including the scalps of Matthew Hayden and Damien Martyn who between them now have more than 150 Test caps.

In the end, he took a respectable 62 wickets at a shade under 26 and with an economy rate of 3.46, more than useful considering he played mostly one-day cricket. Dwyer was a passionate and tenacious cricketer who dug deep while bowling, worked hard on his fielding and he was a player who thought a lot about the game. He was capable of losing his sense of humour when he felt his teammates were putting anything less than everything towards the cause. And he didn't shy away from telling them so.

Although he rarely batted anywhere but No.10 or 11 for Ireland, he was capable of holding up an end with a solid defence. In later years the left-hander would often open the batting for his club. He had a good eye and often got The Hills off to a flyer in one-day games by going over the in-field, scoring a quick 40 or 50 while the early restrictions were still in operation. He put on an unbeaten 24 for the tenth wicket with then captain Angus Dunlop against South Africa at Castle Avenue, Dublin in 1998, enabling Dunlop to reach his century in the process.

Now retired from senior cricket, Dwyer has turned his hand to coaching and is assistant coach to Adrian Birrell with the national side. An affable but no-nonsense operator who takes his job very seriously, he fits well into the more professional-style structure of the current Irish set-up. Depending on whether the Irish Cricket Union continues its policy of choosing overseas candidates for the post of national coach, Dwyer could find himself in the mix for the job at some stage in the future should he decide to go for it.

Ryan Logan Eagleson

RHB, RAM; Carrickfergus, Derbyshire and Ireland (1995-2004)

Ryan Eagleson, a bustling pace bowler from Carrickfergus, caught the attention of coaches in the English County Championship but a serious back injury dogged his career and forced him into retirement before he could really establish himself at that level.

He was just twenty when he first broke onto the scene for Ireland, taking a wicket in his first game against the Earl of Arundel's XI in 1995. Always aggressive, always capable of mixing up pace and line, Eagleson was a feel bowler who, on his day, could trouble full-time professional batsmen with his variation and pace.

A big man who stood 6ft 3ins with a barrel chest, Eagleson's extra height and power surprised a lot of batsmen but in some ways it proved his downfall and with constant pressure being put on his muscles and limbs he often broke down.

He reached his peak in 1999, taking 4 for 59 against Leicestershire at Castle Avenue and was offered terms at Derbyshire where he was highly rated. But his inability to stay fit meant his county career never blossomed and he was out of action for pretty much the entire 2000 season.

He came back in 2001 and was included in the Ireland squad for the ICC Trophy in Canada,

Born: 17 December 1974, Carrickfergus, County Antrim

Batting

Mts	Inns	NOs	Runs
65	45	16	380
Avg	50s	100s	Cts
13.10	1	-	25

Bowling

O	M	R	W
534	52	2,356	70
Avg	5WI	10WM	
33.66	-	-	

Highest score: 50 not out v Scotland, Boghall Linlithgow 1996
Best bowling: 4-59 v Leicestershire, Castle Avenue 1999

a selection that turned out to be a mistake. He started reasonably well against the USA (2-34 off nine overs) and Hong Kong (1-48 off ten) but he was never really fit and finally broke down in Toronto after just two overs against the United Arab Emirates. There were also suggestions that another squad member was selected while not fully fit and a couple of them played a limited role in the competition. And when batsman Decker Curry went home after an altercation with national coach Ken Rutherford, Ireland were down to just eleven players for the last two games of the tournament. Journalist James Fitzgerald was called out of the press tent as a sub fielder in the remaining matches against the Netherlands and host Canada.

Eagleson did not play for Ireland again until the end of the 2003 season and never really recaptured the form of the late 1990s. In the end he played for Ireland sixty-five times, putting him into the top twenty of most capped Irish players. An outgoing and affable character who enjoyed the use of a good mirror, he was always a central personality on Irish tours. He was part of a strong Northern Ireland team that competed in the 1998 Commonwealth Games at Kuala Lumpur

and continues to play for his club Carrickfergus in the Northern Cricket Union leagues, the only Carrick player to come through the junior ranks and play for Ireland. He spent several winters coaching in Hong Kong and he represented Hong Kong in the HK Sixes tournament in 2003 and 2004. He also appeared in an underwear advertisement for Calvin Klein in that part of the world. Back home, he is now a part-time cricket development officer in Northern Ireland.

Although selected as a bowler, Eagleson was also a more than useful lower-order batsman, whose Ireland average of just over 13 does not reflect what he was capable of with the bat in hand. In his debut first-class match in 1996, against Scotland at Boghall Linlithgow, he made 50 not out and 41 not out in a drawn game and has scored two senior centuries for his club.

Eagleson was one of the 'nearly' players of Irish cricket, extremely talented but with a frame that could not handle the rough and tumble of the modern game.

John Watson George Elder

RHB, RAM; Bangor and Ireland (1973-87)

Born: 16 August 1949, Bangor, County Down

Batting

Mts	Inns	NOs	Runs
37	23	8	80
Avg	50s	100s	Cts
5.33	-	-	14

Bowling

O	M	R	W
704.1	222	1,727	70
Avg	5WI	10WM	
24.67	5	-	

Highest score: 28 v Wales, Marchwiel 1979
Best bowling: 6-29 v Denmark, Rathmines 1978

A smiling assassin with the air of a benevolent cousin, the tall, loose-limbed John Elder often surprised his victims with the transformation that took place once he started his run-up. Beneath his affable exterior there beat the big heart of an aggressive competitor, one who took his bowling extremely seriously and was entirely committed to the team cause.

What he lacked in panache and guile he made up for with his wholehearted endeavour. He developed a redoubtable partnership with fellow pace bowler Simon Corlett as the spearhead of the Irish attack during the late 1970s and early '80s. While Corlett was perhaps faster and more technically correct, Elder's added height (he stands 6ft 4ins) issued a different type of challenge to the batsman by generating considerable bounce even on a placid pitch.

Having taken 5 for 41 in Ulster Country's seven-wicket win over North Leinster in 1973, Elder was called up for his first cap, a three-day game against Wales at Rathmines. Ireland won the match in two days and a 40-over game was arranged against the same opposition the fol-

lowing day. Elder took 6 for 15 in seven overs in that uncapped match as Wales were routed for 102.

In the following game, he took 5 for 33 against Denmark and looked to have a very promising international career ahead of him. But he was not always favoured by selectors during a time when opening bowlers were not in short supply. Troubled by shoulder injury and eye problems in the latter part of his career he missed out on some caps that he would have been selected for had he been fully fit.

In total he was capped on thirty-seven occasions, taking 70 wickets at an average of just under 25 with best figures of 6 for 29 against Denmark in 1978.

He was once described by the late Sean Pender, former cricket correspondent in *The Irish Times* as 'blissfully useless with the bat', a comment Elder did not agree with but one he has not been able to refute by pointing to statistics. In total he scored just 80 runs for Ireland in 23 innings at an average of 5.33, hitting no fours but interestingly, one six. He once famously left Ivan Anderson stranded not out on 198 by getting out before the Waringstown batsman could become the first Ireland player to make a double hundred.

Since his retirement from representative cricket in 1987, Elder turned his considerable talents to administration. He has served the Irish Cricket Union as chairman of its cricket committee and also as a national selector. Today he owns and runs a range of cricket websites, including the very popular CricketEurope site, the go-to source for any news, views and statistics about the game in Ireland, Scotland, the Netherlands and beyond.

Francis Fee
RHB, OB; Queen's University, Cregagh and Ireland (1956-59)

Born: 14 May 1934, Belfast.

Batting

Mts	Inns	NOs	Runs
13	18	2	132
Avg	50s	100s	Cts
8.25	-	-	6

Bowling

O	M	R	W
334.3	98	729	58
Avg	5WI	10WM	
12.57	4	3	

Highest score: 31 v New Zealand, Omeau 1958

Best bowling: 9-26 v Scotland, College Park 1957

Frank Fee had the most extraordinary introduction to first-class cricket of any Irish bowler. After two such games he had aggregated 26 wickets at an average of 6.15. In the long history of the game worldwide no one had ever started his first-class career with such a haul.

His debut for Ireland, against Sussex at Rathmines, was not ranked as first class and Fee only bowled two overs before the game was abandoned. One week later he came on after nine overs as first change against MCC at College Park. The tall off-spinner wreaked havoc and bowled unchanged until the visitors were bowled out for 135 and he had the analysis of 24-8-56-7. Ireland were riddled for 48 (GH Chesterton 7-14) before Fee struck again. His return of 28-11-44-7 gave him match figures of 14-100, beaten only for Ireland by 14-97 by Scott Huey against the same opponents, on the same ground, two years before. Fee's return was only beaten by one other debutant anywhere in the twentieth century.

The following summer he played against the West Indian tourists in Ormeau and College Park (4-61, including Frank Worrell and Garfield Sobers), before returning to the Trinity ground for Scotland's visit. Again it was a match dominated by spin and Fee was even more dominant. Scots spinner David Livingston took 6-33 and 5-18 but Fee trumped that with 9-26 and 3-34. Ireland made 139 and 73 to Scotland's 82 and 92. The highest individual score was 30 and the Scottish keeper James Brown equalled the world record of seven dismissals (four catches and three stumpings) in an innings. Later that summer he had another ten-wicket haul, against the Free Foresters at Rathmines, taking 4-36 and 6-19.

It was never the same again for Fee, and his last six caps over the next two seasons yielded only 15 wickets, and despite an economy rate of 2.18 and strike rate of a wicket every 34.6 balls, he played his last game for Ireland aged twenty-five. His decline is still hailed as a mystery, although one knowledgeable observer points out that Fee was the victim of his club's dearth of opening bowlers. Cregagh, an unfashionable East Belfast side, were strong in the 1950s but were short of quickies. Fee was prevailed upon to set aside his off-spin in the service of his club and his Ireland form suffered. The Irish selectors became reluctant to pick him as he was no longer practising his art and a glittering career ended far too early.

James Blandford Ganly

RHB, RFM; Leinster, Dublin University, Phoenix and Ireland (1921-37)

100 GREATS

Jim Ganly was a strong, powerfully built all-rounder who has attained legendary status between the wars for the power of his hitting and his speed between the wickets. This speed and power was honed on the rugby fields, where he played with Monkstown and won twelve caps on the wing for Ireland from 1927-30, scoring seven tries.

Educated at St Columba's, Ganly was reputedly given detention on the weekend of internationals to ensure he played for school ahead of country. He entered Trinity in January 1922 already a first-class cricketer, but spent just two seasons there, scoring more than 1,000 runs in that time, including two brisk centuries against Civil Service. A 'free, forward-playing batsman and a hitter of big, lofty drives', in 1923 and 1926 he won the Marchant Cup for the province's best average.

In all he made eleven competitive centuries, all with great speed and belligerence. The fastest, an unbeaten 108, (5 sixes, 9 fours) came in forty-five minutes against Phoenix at Rathmines in 1926. He had made 86 in the first innings of the two-day game. He is the only man to make two double centuries in Leinster, 203 against Trinity at Rathmines in 1927, and a brilliant 232 in just two hours in the 1929 league final against Phoenix. He hit 192 in boundaries that day (6 sixes, 39 fours), bringing up his first hundred in fifty minutes by hitting 22 in one over.

He won five league medals in succession with Leinster (1928-32) before moving to Phoenix, with whom he won a league in 1936 and cup in 1937 (4-22 in the final).

Ganly was in and out of the Ireland side until 1925 when he made 62* against Scotland to set up victory. He first captained the following season, marking it with 58 against Wales. He was passed over as captain for the next few games – he made four 50s in five innings including 83 and 68 v MCC – before taking charge for the visit of the 1928 West Indians.

It was to be his greatest day, as he led Ireland from the front to a spectacular win – still the only win over a Test nation in a first-class match.

Born: 7 March 1904, Dublin
Died: 22 July 1976, Oughterard, County Galway

Batting

Mts	Inns	NOs	Runs	HS
25	44	2	831	83

Avg	50s	100s	Cts
19.79	6	-	10

Bowling

O	M	R	W	Avg
66	14	239	9	26.56

5WI	10WM
-	-

Highest innings: 83 v MCC, College Park 1926
Best bowling: 2-22 v Scotland, College Park 1927

He recalled the 'exciting and memorable' day in an article for the programme for Ireland v West Indies in 1976, a match which took place six days before his death. 'I knew our fielding would be first class by any standards, the bowling was steady but not very hostile... and the batting always a little suspect.' Ganly contributed vital runs – 43 and 31 – to the famous victory.

He captained Ireland on eight occasions, winning only twice, including his final game in charge against the Catamarans in 1929. Typical of the eccentric selection at the time, he was dropped in 1930 after top scoring against Cahn's XI and came back for one more cap in 1934 against MCC.

The *Leinster Cricket Annual* described him in 1941 as 'addicted to tremendous, high straight drives'. Another witness maintained that even the greatest of bowlers feared him in full flight. He was a useful bowler but rarely got to bowl for Ireland, especially when he wasn't captain. He won the all-rounder trophy in Leinster in 1928.

His last two centuries – which each took an hour – came in successive innings against Clontarf and Civil service in 1937. He retired in 1939 with 5,523 league and cup runs at an average of 31. He was elected president of the Irish Cricket Union in 1965 and was a well-known cattle dealer and auctioneer. He was found dead from a gunshot wound having gone out shooting alone in Co. Galway in 1976.

Peter Gerard Gillespie
RHB, RAM; Strabane and Ireland (1995-)

Born: 11 May 1974, Strabane

Batting

Mts	Inns	NOs	Runs
114	113	19	2,599
Avg	**50s**	**100s**	**Cts**
27.65	18	1	30

Bowling

O	M	R	W
151.4	15	672	18
Avg	**5WI**	**10WM**	
37.33	-	-	

Highest score: 102 not out v MCC, Upritchard Park, Bangor 2005
Best bowling: 3-42 v Hong Kong, Kuala Lumpur 1997

Peter Gillespie is what national coach Adrian Birrell calls 'the heartbeat of the team'. A hugely popular member of the squad, Gillespie is one of six men to have played more than one hundred times for the country (the others being Kyle McCallan, Alan Lewis, Garfield Harrison, Angus Dunlop and Stephen Warke), and the most-capped player from the North-West.

He came into the team in 1995 as a right-arm medium-pace bowler who batted in the lower middle order but a nagging shoulder injury and a determination to improve his batting meant that his role shifted to that of a free-scoring middle-order batsman who occasionally turned the arm over. Indeed, when he came on to bowl against the United Arab Emirates in the 2005 ICC Intercontinental Cup semi-final, it was the first time in nearly five and a half years that he had done so while wearing Irish colours.

On the international scene he will probably be most remembered as being a cool head in a crisis. He seemed to specialise in rescuing Ireland innings from disaster with four or five wickets down and not many runs on the board.

Needing 239 to win against Canada in the 2005 ICC Trophy semi-final at Clontarf, Gillespie came in with Ireland struggling at 106 for 5. Batting first with Trent Johnston and then Andy White, the Strabane man made an unbeaten 64 to see the side home with four wickets and four balls to spare. And in 2006 he made a vital 41 not out on a difficult pitch against Gloucestershire in a C&G Trophy match at Bristol. Coming in at 96 for 5, Gillespie's knock made sure Ireland posted what turned out to be a winning total of 193. It was the first time Ireland had beaten a county side away from home in any one-day competition.

He also made Ireland's quickest ever century against the MCC at Upritchard Park, Bangor in 2005. A six over deep backward square off the last ball of the innings and just the 47th he faced, brought him to an unbeaten 102, his first century for Ireland. His elder brother Mark won four caps as an all-rounder for Ireland and in some ways was a more effective cricketer at club level than Peter, particularly in the 1990s. A laid-back character, Peter had been criticised for getting good starts but then throwing his wicket away but he worked hard on his technique and later became known as a player who carefully built an innings before taking any risks.

It took him a while to establish himself in the team and he was controversially left out of the squad for the 2001 ICC Trophy in Canada. It is something that then captain Kyle McCallan now realises was a mistake.

'For Peter Gillespie not to go to Toronto was hara-kiri,' says McCallan. 'That is one of my biggest regrets because I was involved in that decision-making process. I deeply regret that he wasn't there.'

But Gillespie worked hard, bided his time and fought his way back into the team. He now maintains that it took his omission from that ICC Trophy side to make the necessary transition into an out-and-out batsman and find his niche within the team.

A civil servant based in Derry, he rarely misses a team training session despite having to make a six-hour round trip from the North-West to the main training centre in north County Dublin.

He won his one-hundredth cap for Ireland against Glamorgan at Sophia Gardens in 2006, ten days before his thirty-second birthday, making a half-century in the process. By that stage he had asserted himself as a vital member of the squad.

'He gives his heart and soul to Irish cricket and is very passionate about it,' said Birrell. 'He is very reliable in the middle order, more and more so as he gets older. An intelligent cricketer, I have a very high regard for him as a player and also as a personality.'

100
G R E A T S

Douglas Edward Goodwin
RHB, RAM; Malahide and Ireland (1965-75)

The name of Dougie Goodwin will always be associated in Irish cricket circles and perhaps further afield, with the famous day in 1969 when Ireland humbled the West Indians by bowling them out for just 25 on a green pitch at Sion Mills. Wisden later called it 'the sensation' of the season and the day after the remarkable match the *Daily Mirror* ran a front page headline 'Supermen' over a large picture of Goodwin and fellow opening bowler Alec O'Riordan. Several other newspapers, such as the *London Times* and *Daily Mail* had front-page pieces on it while it dominated the back pages of the *Belfast News Letter*, *Evening Herald* and *Evening Press*.

Understandably, people have always felt a need to explain this extraordinary feat. There have been rumours since then that the West Indians partied too hard the night before, having been introduced to Guinness and Irish Mist by the canny Irish. But as with most conspiracy theories, the truth is probably a lot more simple and perhaps a little duller. On a helpful wicket, medium-pacers Goodwin and O'Riordan bowled beautifully. The Irish team, especially Gerry Duffy in the gully, fielded magnificently. And the West Indians, tired from having just finished a Test match against England at Lord's the day before, played poor shots in what was a humiliating experience for them.

'Coming from Lord's, that would have been a bit of a change,' Goodwin told journalist Peter Breen. 'Every ball that was hit in the air found an Irish pair of hands.' Goodwin's figures that day were 12.3-8-6-5 while O'Riordan took 4-18 and there was one run out. In the second innings Goodwin had figures of 2-1 meaning that he took as many wickets (seven) in the match as runs were scored off him.

Born: 2 May 1938, Dublin

Batting

Mts	Inns	NOs	Runs
43	52	12	494
Avg	50s	100s	Cts
12.35	-	-	25

Bowling

O	M	R	W
1134.4	420	2,551	115
Avg	5WI	10WM	
22.18	6	1	

Highest score: 41 v Mr Wilfred Isaac's XI, Rathmines 1969
Best bowling: 7-39 v Combined Services, Shane Park 1968

But it would be a mistake to reduce Goodwin's career to one glorious occasion because this was not a fluke. He remains one of Ireland's best opening bowlers of any era. His 115 wickets came at an average of 22.18 and he maintained an impressive economy rate throughout his career of 2.25 per over.

A steady-paced bowler of metronomic accuracy, on slower Irish pitches, more given to lateral movement, Goodwin had few equals. The end of his Ireland career coincided with the start of Bangor opening bowler John Elder, who was quite in awe of what Goodwin could do with the ball.

'I played with Dougie for one year and marvelled at his wonderful control,' said Elder. 'He's the sort of bowler that youngsters should

be able to watch to learn what good bowling is all about and how to do it.'

Goodwin's best bowling for Ireland came against the Combined Services at Shane Park, Belfast in 1968. He took 7-39 in the first innings, followed up with 4-13 in the second as Ireland won by 46 runs for what was his only ten-wicket match in Ireland colours. He did, however, manage a total of six five-wicket innings, including 5-68 against the touring Australians at Ormeau, Belfast in July 1968.

He captained Ireland on nineteen occasions, registering seven wins and four defeats, making him one of the more successful skippers Ireland have had, but leading Ireland to victory over the West Indies in 1969 will surely rank as his greatest achievement as a player.

William Robert Gregory
RHB, LBG; Co Galway, Phoenix and Ireland (1912)

Born: 20 May 1881, Coole Park, Gort, Co. Galway

Died: 23 January 1918, near Grossa, Padua, Italy

Batting

Mts	Inns	NOs	Runs
1	2	0	0

Avg	50s	100s	Cts
0.00	0	0	0

O	M	R	W
27	3	92	9

Avg	5WI	10WM
10.22	1	0

Best bowling: 8-80 v Scotland, Rathmines, 1912

Robert Gregory is best remembered for his illustrious mother, his multi-faceted life, his gallant death and the poems he inspired WB Yeats to write. But this excellent all-round sportsman was also a cricketer and on the only occasion he played for Ireland took an incredible 8-80, still one of the top-forty debut performances in all first-class cricket.

Gregory came from cricketing stock; his uncle Robert Persse played for the 20 of Ireland against the United South of England in 1865, making the second-highest score of 17. William Robert Gregory was born at Coole Park, Co. Galway to Persse's sister, Augusta in 1881. Lady Gregory, a noted playwright, was a promoter of the Irish literary revival and founder of the Abbey Theatre.

Coole Park was a centre of literary and artistic endeavour – Robert's paintings are still highly prized – and the only child grew up in a fascinating environment. WB Yeats, JM Synge and Augustus John were frequent guests, while WG Grace visited for the fishing and shooting. Robert played cricket on the lawn at home – in one of the many games featuring the guests, George Bernard Shaw insisted that a member of staff chase the ball for him when he fielded.

Robert took up the game at Harrow, and also played at New College, Oxford. He excelled at boxing (Oxford blue and French amateur champion), shooting and riding.

He played regularly for Galway and after joining Phoenix was picked for Ireland against Scotland at Rathmines in 1912. It turned out to be one of the most remarkable debuts.

The Scots won the toss and batted, reaching 29-0 when George Meldon tossed the ball to Gregory. Bowling medium-paced leg-breaks and cutters, he ran through the Scottish order, returning figures of 23-2-80-8 as the visitors collapsed to 147. Ireland made 98 (Gregory 0) and when the Scots were bowled out for 83 (Gregory 1-12) the target was set at 133. Ireland fell four runs short, with Gregory completing his pair, a disappointing end to a brilliant debut. Ireland played just two more games before the war and Gregory wasn't selected for either.

He worked in Jacques Blanche's design studio and had his own exhibition of paintings in

Chelsea in 1914. In 1915 he joined up with the 4th Connaught Rangers, transferring to the Royal Flying Corps in 1916. He won the award of Chevalier of the Legion d'Honneur and the Military Cross 'for conspicuous gallantry and devotion to duty'. He recorded nineteen 'kills' and is also believed to have shot down the famous 'Red Baron' von Richthofen, who survived. Gregory died the following day at the age of thirty-seven in the skies above Padua when an Italian pilot mistakenly shot him down.

Yeats wrote four powerful poems about him: 'An Irish Airman Foresees His Death', 'In Memory of Major Robert Gregory', 'Shepherd and Goatherd', and 'Reprisals'.

Lucius Henry Gwynn — 100 GREATS
RHB, RM; Dublin University, Phoenix and Ireland (1892-1902)

Born: 5 May 1873, Ramelton, Co. Donegal
Died: 23 December 1902, Davos Platz, Switzerland

Batting

Mts	Inns	NOs	Runs
11	15	2	499
Avg	50s	100s	Cts
38.38	5	-	6

O	M	R	W
120	46	254	14
Avg	5WI	10WM	
18.14	-	-	

Highest score: 81* v London County, Crystal Palace 1902
Best bowling: 4-64 v Surrey, The Oval 1895

Lucius Gwynn was a batting all-rounder who played just eleven times for Ireland, but deserves to be called the finest Irish cricketer of the nineteenth century. His short career ended with 499 runs at 38.38, the best average until Alf Masood in the 1980s. His exploits for Ireland, for Dublin University against county sides, and for the Gentlemen against the Players may even have brought him close to a Test cap.

He came from a large and remarkable family: his eldest brother, Stephen, was a prolific writer and nationalist MP. The fifth son, Arthur, won cricket and rugby caps, while Robin played rugby for Leinster and cricket for Ireland. John was a fine player at Trinity who went to India and played first-class cricket for the Europeans in the Madras tournament.

At St Columba's, between 1885-90, and for the early part of his time in Trinity, Gwynn was first and foremost a bowler. He scored his first century for Trinity, 143 against the Curragh Brigade, in 1893, the season that saw him established as a leading all-rounder with 44 wickets at 8.14. It was one of the greatest seasons in the history of the club, with ten wins and two draws recorded – including wins over Oxford University, Leicestershire, Warwickshire (who were bowled out for 15) and a draw with Essex.

Lucius was elected captain for 1894 and again in 1895, ironically the two least successful seasons for the club in all his time there. That record is probably due to the high calibre of fixtures those summers – they played Cambridge twice, South Africa, Gloucestershire, MCC and Leicestershire.

The year of 1895 was an epic one in cricket history and was to be Gwynn's biggest year too: *Wisden* shows the young Irishman astride the national batting averages with 455 at an average of 56 – five runs more than W G Grace. Trinity toured England, and Lucius kicked off with 63 and 106 at Cambridge, and carried his bat to 153* and 24 at Leicester. Gwynn was also the best bowler as Trinity were heavily defeated in both games, taking 4-93 in Fenner's, and 3-43 and 4-81 at Grace Road.

Gwynn played several other games in England that summer: 10 and 63 for Ireland v Surrey at the Oval, 80 for Ireland v MCC on his first visit to Lord's, and 80 and 0 for Gentlemen v Players at the Oval. Gwynn was selected for the latter on the personal recommendation of Grace, who described him as 'one of the most finished bats I have ever played against'.

Gwynn let down neither himself nor Irish cricket as he top scored in the Gentlemen's first innings of 320. He added 135 with CB Fry, facing two all-time great bowlers in Tom Richardson and George Lohmann. *The Times* wrote: 'He has a steady and finished style, which yesterday he exercised for three hours

and a quarter. His defence, too, came at an opportune time for the Gentlemen, who did badly at the start, and it was his batting which laid the foundations for the big total.' Gwynn eventually 'threw away his wicket' going for a short run – his batting partner at the time was said to be hard of hearing, as was Gwynn. The next summer he was invited back, but made just 24 and 1.

He made three hundreds in College Park in 1896, kicking off with 120 v MCC and then making 178 v Leinster and 100 v Co. Kildare. That summer was to prove his best for the club, becoming only the second man after Comyn (1,174 in 1895) to score a thousand runs, while also chipping in with 93 wickets at 9.73.

That summer saw the most mysterious event of Gwynn's cricket career. It was reported in *The Irish Times* that Lucius had been selected by the Lancashire committee to represent England in the Second Test at Old Trafford. It was later written that he would be unable to turn out due to scholarship examinations in Trinity and his place was to be taken by the Indian prince, Ranjitsinhji. He finished his Trinity career in

1897 with 3,195 runs at almost 33 (8 centuries), and 311 wickets at 11.33.

Gwynn was not a big man, being described as 'almost delicate' at about 5ft 9ins and eleven stone. Stephen Gwynn described his brother batting thus:'I remember seeing Lucius bat once on the Leinster ground, which is very narrow; and the bowler sent down a short one, which he pulled across, low to mid on, without any special appearance of putting his weight into it. But I never saw a cricket ball travel so hard.'

Gwynn's play off the back foot 'rivalled Ranjitsinjhi', according to Pat Hone, who remembered him for his 'glorious straight drives, and the combination of predominantly back play in defence, with quick-footed driving in attack, which is a mark of the highest flights of batsmanship'.

His eleven Irish caps were spread over a decade. He went on the tour of England in 1902 although he was unavailable for the second half of the tour. He was persuaded to play against a weak London County side and against MCC at Lord's, where he made 11 and 5 in a rainy draw.

Lucius played throughout the 1902 season while feeling unwell. It is a mark of the man that, for club and country, he scored over 1,000 runs at 50 and made four consecutive centuries on the Phoenix ground. That autumn, with his health declining rapidly, his doctors sent him to a Harley Street specialist who diagnosed tuberculosis. He had been married less than two years and his daughter Rhoda was born that September.

He travelled to a Swiss sanatorium with his sister Lucy, where two days before Christmas he died. *The Irish Times* carried an editorial:'Surely, never before has a career opened so brightly and closed so suddenly... Lucius Gwynn's career awoke unbounded admiration amongst his fellows and of envy or jealousy no trace.' *Wisden* also printed a tribute: 'There can be little doubt that if he had had regular opportunities of playing in first-class matches in England he would have earned a high place among the batsmen of his day.'

He also won seven rugby caps and in 1894 was part of the Irish team that won the Triple Crown for the first time.

Michael Halliday ———————————————————— 100
RHB, RAO; Phoenix, Dublin University and Ireland (1970-89)   G R E A T S

Undoubtedly the finest Irish right-arm off-spinner of his generation, Mike Halliday won ninety-three caps – twenty-five of them as captain – between 1970 and 1989 and remains the seventh most-capped Ireland player. Able to turn the ball on even the truest of surfaces, Halliday was a genuine spinner who could trouble the very best batsmen on his day.

His performance against Middlesex at Lord's in the 1980 Gillette Cup still ranks as one of the finest individual displays by an Irishman. Defending an impossibly low total of 102 all out, there was no way Ireland could actually win the game but with figures of 4-22 off 12 overs with such notable scalps as Mike Gatting,

Mike Brearley, Roland Butcher and Clive Radley, the right-arm Dubliner at least stole some of the column inches in the newspapers the next day. At one stage Middlesex were 67 for 5.

'Middlesex were embarrassed, not to say mesmerised, by the bowling of Michael Halliday,' wrote John Woodcock in *The Times* of London. 'The way they played him brought to mind England's playing of Ramadhin thirty years ago. I am not saying that he is a better bowler than (John) Emburey but on this occasion he was certainly the more puzzling one.'

After that same game, the great England spinner Jim Laker remarked: 'That was an out-

Born: 20 August 1948, Dublin

Mts	Inns	NOs	Runs
93	81	33	724
Avg	50s	100s	Cts
15.08	1	-	25

O	M	R	W
1961.2	474	5,819	192
Avg	5WI	10WM	
30.31	5	2	

Highest score: 62 not out v MCC, Castle Avenue 1986
Best bowling: 7-58 v MCC, Eglinton 1978

standing exhibition of off-spin, the best I have seen for quite a while.'

While still a student at Dublin University, Halliday made his debut for Ireland in 1970 and took a while to establish himself in the side – he didn't take a wicket until the second innings of his third game and in the five matches that summer of 1970 he took just three at a cost of more than 80 runs apiece. But it was clear that Halliday was a bowler of real talent and selectors' faith was rewarded in time as he managed to hone his skill through hard work and experience.

In his ninety-three caps, he took 192 wickets – the fifth most by an Irishman. He took five wickets in an innings on five occasions and ten wickets in a match twice. While his bowling was what he was selected for, his batting improved immensely as he got older and although he averaged not much more than 15 with the bat, he was capable of doing a very competent job for the team when the chips were down. Against the West Indians, he made and excellent 43 at Rathmines in 1984. He scored 62 not out (bat-

ting at number ten) and 45 (having put himself up the order to six) against the MCC at Castle Avenue in 1986 and also seemed to reserve his best batting when playing old rivals Scotland, not least the memorable knocks he had in both innings at Dumfries in 1988. That match against the MCC was memorable for the performance of a young Australian, Mark Waugh, who scored an unbeaten 239 and 101 not out with only Halliday managing to avoid serious damage to his bowling figures.

Halliday's captaincy was less celebrated than his other on-field exploits. He was criticised for being too conservative and his record of four wins from twenty-five matches at the helm was certainly not particularly impressive. It didn't help of course that he lost 19 of 25 tosses as captain, including 14 in a row at one stage, and he did lead Ireland against some very strong teams during that period.

He is the most successful club cricketer ever in Leinster, winning sixteen cup or league titles with Phoenix and another league with Dublin University. He also won the Irish Senior Cup with Phoenix in 1986, taking 3-13 in the final against Donemana. In 435 senior club matches, he took 983 wickets at less than 15, including 55 five-wicket hauls.

He retired from representative cricket at the end of the 1989 season, just one week after his forty-first birthday. At that stage he still had the fitness and form to continue and surely could have become Ireland's first player to reach one hundred caps. In any event, he had nothing left to prove and he still remains one of Ireland's finest cricketers of any era.

Blayney Balfour Hamilton
RHB, SLA; Phoenix, Dundrum and Ireland (1891-1907)

100 GREATS

Born: 13 June 1872, Mellifont, Collon, County Louth
Died: 16 December 1946, Dublin

Batting

Mts	Inns	NOs	Runs
19	28	2	490
Avg	50s	100s	Cts
18.85	2	-	21

Bowling

O	M	R	W
602	176	1436	95
Avg	5WI	10WM	
15.12	7	2	

Highest innings: 80 v All New York, Staten Island, 1892
Best bowling: 6-33 v I Zingari, Phoenix CC, 1894

Blayney 'Bud' Hamilton was a gifted all-round sportsman who represented Ireland at four sports, most notably cricket. He won one hockey cap in 1896, and also represented his country at badminton and tennis, as well as being the leading rackets player in Ireland for many years. The Hamiltons were an extraordinary family, with four sons representing Ireland at cricket (3), soccer (2), tennis (2), badminton (1) and hockey (1). Willoughby, a soccer international, won the Men Singles Championship at Wimbledon in 1890.

Blayney was educated in England at Haileybury College, where he excelled at cricket and rackets. He was still in his teens when he was first capped against I Zingari in the Phoenix Park. A left-arm spinner, he bowled slowly and turned the ball both ways – 'very crafty' was how Pat Hone described him. He usually batted for Ireland in the top six, but his average of 18.85 does not do him justice. He was described by contemporaries as a first-rate batsman, but Hone reckoned 'possibly he did not bother enough; all games came too easy to him'. He recalled an I

Zingari player at the Vice-Regal Lodge saying he thought Bud was the best natural cricketer he had ever seen. He had several important innings for Ireland, with his best score of 80 coming against New York on the 1892 tour. He batted with grit against All Philadelphia, holding the tail together for as long as he could in making 38 but when he was out to the lethal Bart King defeat ensued and the series was drawn.

He was a star of that tour, taking 29 wickets in eight innings and being summed up by the *American Cricketer* magazine thus: 'Hamilton is an excellent bowler'. He took wickets a phenomenal rate, each of his 95 wickets coming every 39 balls, at an average of just over 15. He took six wickets in an innings on six occasions, twice against I Zingari in 1894 when he returned 12-109 in the match, including England players O'Brien and Leveson-Gower twice. Two years later he took 10-130 against MCC at Rathmines and 6-51 to defeat IZ by an innings.

Ireland had a sparse fixture list at the time and did not play again for three years. Hamilton was overlooked in 1899 but played in the next fixture, against the 1901 South Africans. He returned for one more cap, against the same opponents in 1907 but finished his Ireland career five short of 100 wickets.

His fielding was also of the highest order. Jack Meldon recalled a catch Hamilton made in their second match at Philadelphia 'Bud was on at one end, Archie Penny at the other. Penny was renowned for his slow long-hops at times... I always fielded Bud at cover-point where he was a sort of Jessop. The long-hop was duly dealt with but about eight feet off the ground Bud got a hand to it; the sound was like a pistol shot and the ball stuck. The finest catch I ever witnessed.'

He was also responsible for one of the most incredible games ever seen in Dublin, when Dundrum bowled out Pembroke for 4. Hamilton finished with figures of 4.3-4-0-5 and Lucius Gwynn 4-4-1-5.

In 1898 he married Irene Long and, with his brother Willoughby, founded the auctioneering firm Hamilton and Hamilton.

100
GREATS

William Drummond Hamilton
LHB; Leinster, Dundrum, Oxford University and Ireland (1883-96)

Drummond Hamilton was one of four members of a prominent family who played for Ireland over a period from 1877 to 1907. His cousin Horace was first to be capped, with a career highlight of 7-15 and 4-78 against I Zingari in 1878. He won eight caps – and broke the Canadian high jump record while on tour with Ireland – but died suddenly while playing billiards aged thirty-six. Drummond was the eldest of three brothers; Rev. FCL (Lowry) won four caps from 1888-93 and Blayney (see previous page) nineteen from 1891-1907.

Drummond's final haul of caps was a modest 14 – Ireland played thirty-six games in that time but Hamilton was not always available, missing the tours to North America in 1888 and 1892 for example. But he showed enough quality in those fourteen games to rank among the best batsmen of the nineteenth century.

He was educated in England at Haileybury, where he was in the first XI in 1876 and 1877. The school yearbook described him as: 'A thoroughly good left-handed bat, who always plays the game and hits well to all parts of the field; a capital point.' He went up to Queen's College, Oxford.

In 1880 he made 211 not out against University College. In 1882 he scored 109★ against Corpus Christi and was selected for the University XI. With 53 under his belt against the Gentlemen of England, he played in the Varsity Match at Lord's but was so nervous that he set off

William Drummond Hamilton
continued

Born: 4 May 1859, Mellifont, Collon, Co Louth
Died: 4 March 1914, Park Town, Oxford

Batting

Mts	Inns	NOs	Runs
14	18	-	505
Avg	**50s**	**100s**	**Cts**
28.06	4	-	9

Highest score: 93 v I Zingari, Phoenix Park 1896

for a run in the wrong direction. He made 9 and 0 for his side which included fellow Irishmen Edward Shaw and Charles Leslie. Returning to Dublin for the holidays he played five games for Leinster and averaged 34.

Finished at Oxford, he made 54 for MCC against the university at Lord's in 1883, the year he made his debut for Ireland. Against I Zingari at the Phoenix Park he made 28 and 7 but did not play again for four years. The Canadians visited in 1887 and 'with brilliant hitting' made 62 (the first time Ireland made over 300 at home) and 31, while he made another 62 against the Philadelphians in 1889.

South Africa toured Britain and Ireland in 1894 on a non-first-class basis and he made

a classy 68 against them – out of 153 – at Rathmines. His last game for Ireland was in 1896 when he was bowled by Dowson of I Zingari, seven runs short of a century.

Wisden described Hamilton as 'a fine, free left-handed hitter and a beautiful field, especially in the long field', and at his peak he stood 5ft 8ins and weighed ten stone. He married Alice, daughter of George Kinahan, who played in Ireland's first international match in 1855. Drummond later followed his father to become rector of the parish of Taney in Dublin.

A soccer player with Dublin Association, he played once for Ireland against Wales in 1885.

William Harrington

RHB, OB; Leinster, County Kildare and Ireland (1894-1921)

Born: 27 December 1869, Templeogue, County Dublin

Died: 2 January 1940, Templeogue, County Dublin

Batting

Mts	Inns	NOs	Runs	
28	42	10	270	
Avg	HS	50s	100s	Cts
8.44	30	-	-	10

Bowling

O	M	R	W
798.5	223	1862	112
Best	Avg	5WI	10WM
7-76	16.62	8	1

Highest score: 30 v Cambridge University 1904, Rathmines

Best bowling: 7-76 v Cambridge University 1902, Cambridge

Bill Harrington was an incisive off-break bowler whose career spanned the Golden Age, although he continued bowling in Leinster senior cricket until the age of sixty-two. The league was only inaugurated in 1919, when Harrington was in his fiftieth year, but over the next thirteen seasons he captured 331 wickets at 14.06.

Harrington was part of a unique Irish attack which included fellow offies Tom Ross and Bob Lambert. They were quite different bowlers however and formed a lethal combination at times. Harrington was very accurate and flighted the ball with an almost square-arm action delivered from an erect 6ft 2ins frame. *The Irish Field* wrote of him: 'Decidedly slow, he was a real master of his craft. A greater artist never lived at getting a batsman lbw, or by skilful flighting of the ball at luring him to destruction. He bowled a splendid off-break, sometimes varying his deliveries with one that came from leg.'

He was schooled at Mount St Mary in Derbyshire before entering Clongowes at the age of fifteen. There he fell under the coaching of Nottinghamshire cricketers Frank Shacklock and Billy Barnes, and he developed into a fine bowler. Barnes recalled him as 'the best lad bowler I ever saw'.

His twenty-seven-year Ireland career began in 1894 with six wickets against I Zingari, and he was good enough to take four-for in each innings against Surrey at the Oval and 9-36 in the match against MCC at Lord's two years later.

He was unfortunate that Ireland played infrequently in the late nineteenth century – just one game from 1896-1901 – but he was an essential selection for the decade that followed. He never tired and was willing to bowl all day if necessary. Against Cambridge on the 1902 tour he bowled 56 overs on the trot.

That tour was his finest hour, taking 21 wickets in four games, including a career best 7-76 and 4-42 v Cambridge and 5-26 and 3-22 against WG Grace's London County. Against South Africa at the Mardyke in 1904 he took 5-66 and three years later he took 4-79 and 5-48 against them in Trinity.

In 1912, aged forty-two and at his home ground in Rathmines, he riddled the Scottish tail, taking 5-15. He might have expected that to be his international farewell, especially when war broke out, but he was recalled once more in 1921 for the same fixture. Showing plenty of his old guile, he returned figures of 4-26 and 3-11 in a rain-affected draw. Astonishingly, at fifty-one, he still had plenty of cricket in his old bones and only retired after winning his sixth league medal in 1931.

Garfield David Harrison

LHB, RAO; Waringstown and Ireland (1983-1997)

100 GREATS

Born: 8 May 1961, Lurgan

Batting

Mts	Inns	NOs	Runs
118	132	26	2,765
Avg	50s	100s	Cts
26.08	12	1	34

Bowling

O	M	R	W
1332.5	218	4,714	140
Avg	5WI	10WM	
33.67	3	-	

Highest score: 105 not out v Scotland, Hamilton Crescent 1994
Best bowling: 9-113 v Scotland, Myreside 1990

One of four brothers to play for Ireland, Garfield Harrison stood head and shoulders above his siblings in terms of ability and although he was the youngest in the family he quickly established himself as a leading member of the Waringstown club as well as the Harrison clan.

He was a bowling all-rounder who probably would have made the Irish team as a batsman alone and although he will be remembered as one of Ireland's finest off-spinners, he actually began his international career opening the bowling with another legendary figure in the Irish game, Simon Corlett. As such, he was a true all-rounder.

'From the time he was a young boy he wanted to bowl spin,' said his brother Roy, who himself played three times for Ireland and was president of the Irish Cricket Union in 2006. 'But Waringstown needed an opening bowler so he bowled seam-up for the club first team when he was sixteen or seventeen... his first half-dozen matches or so for Ireland were as their opening bowler.'

And although he had a fair measure of success as a quick bowler, it soon became apparent that his real talent was as a deadly accurate off-spinner who wasn't afraid to give the ball a bit of air and a real rip.

In 1990 Ireland played a three-day game against Scotland on a flat track in Edinburgh and although the game ended in a tame draw, it will always be remembered for Harrison's marathon first-innings bowling spell. In 43.2 overs he took nine wickets for 113, which were the best first-class figures in the world that year. They are still the best bowling figures for an Irish player away from home and they put him into an exclusive four-man group of people who have taken nine wickets in an innings for Ireland. The others are Arthur Samuels (in 1859 against I Zingari at the Phoenix Park), Frank Fee (9 for 26 in 1957 against Scotland at College Park) and Thomas Ross (9 for 28 in 1904 against South Africa at the Mardyke).

In an outstanding international career that lasted from 1983 to the end of the ICC Trophy in Kuala Lumpur in 1997, Harrison played 118 times for Ireland, taking 140 wickets, putting him ninth in the all-time list. He has a top score with the bat of 105 not out and still holds the record fourth-wicket partnership of an unbeaten 224 with Alan Lewis against Scotland in 1994.

Always a tough competitor, he captained his beloved Waringstown to the treble of the NCU Cup and League and the Irish Senior Cup in 1992. He was a natural winner and demanded high standards from his teammates.

'He was always encouraging his fellow players but if it was necessary he could give somebody a ripping off for not giving their best. He was the first in the queue for doing that,' said brother Roy.

In a cricket-mad household (he is named after West Indian great Garfield Sobers) it was never doubted that he would be a top player and although as the youngest of six good players he had a lot to live up to, it soon became clear that he would be the best of them all. After retiring from international cricket in 1997 he went on to qualify as a coach and became the Northern Ireland Cricket Association's first development officer, a job since taken over by Brian Walsh.

100 GREATS

James Harrison
RHB; Waringstown and Ireland (1969-77)

Jim Harrison was one of a family dynasty of cricketers who dominated the Waringstown club in Co. Armagh for much of the second half of the twentieth century. Out of six brothers, four ended up playing for Ireland (the others being Roy, Deryck and Garfield).

While Garfield was clearly a much better bowler and fielder, Jim was probably his equal when it came to batting. He scored two international centuries, 111 not out against Wales at Rathmines in 1973 – his first ton in any grade of cricket – and an unbeaten 100 against Scotland in his penultimate match for Ireland at Castle Avenue in 1977.

Having played thirty-two times he retired at the end of that season and although he was thirty-six, there is little doubt that he could have continued longer and that the selectors would have liked him to do so. But commitments with his job in an optical company in Lurgan coupled with his feeling that he wanted to give his younger brother Deryck his chance in the Irish side (Deryck made his debut the following year) led to him calling it a day.

A very correct right-handed batsman, the strong-wristed Harrison had a rock-solid defence and scored a lot of his runs in front of square through the off side. He wasn't so fond of the short stuff, however, and in those days without helmets he was wary of the ball that came near his head. He was an excellent reader

James Harrison
continued

Born: 3 May 1941, Lurgan

Batting

Mts	Inns	NOs	Runs
32	58	5	1,347
Avg	50s	100s	Cts
25.42	4	2	11

Highest score: 111 not out v Wales, Rathmines 1973

of the game and captained Waringstown for two years. But according to his elder brother, Roy, his contribution to the team did not extend much beyond what he did with bat in hand.

'He didn't bowl and he was a poor enough fielder,' said Roy. 'He always tried to hide in the field because he liked sleeping. But whenever he decided the team needed his full attention, you got it maybe for half an hour. You fought for supremacy and then when that was gained, Jimmy went back to sleep again.

'He was a good all-round sportsman. Good at football, an excellent rugby player but a wee bit lazy. Playing cricket for Ireland it used to drive (then captain) Alec O'Riordan mad that Jimmy would disappear down to third man the first chance he got.'

Now retired from work, in January 2006 Harrison left Ireland and emigrated with his wife to Sydney, Australia, to be closer to their only son and granddaughter.

Derek Heasley
RHB, RAM; Lisburn, Glendermott, CIYMS and Ireland (1996-2002)

100 GREATS

An honest all-rounder with a good attitude towards the game, Derek Heasley played sixty times for Ireland during what was a difficult time for Irish cricket in the late 1990s and into the new millennium. He made an encouraging start to his international career in 1996 and showed that nerves were not something that troubled him unduly.

In his first match against Surrey, in the Benson & Hedges Cup at Eglinton, he found himself walking to the wicket with the score on 17 for 5 with a possible rout on the cards against a side that included England players Alec Stewart, Chris Lewis, Graham Thorpe, Adam and Ben Hollioake and Australian left-arm fast bowler Brendan Julian. Undeterred, he rapidly added 45 for the sixth wicket with Neil Doak, of which his share was 36. He also snaffled the wicket of Thorpe in that match, caught behind by Alan Rutherford, and finished with figures of 1-32 off seven overs.

Born: 15 January 1972, Lisburn

Batting

Mts	Inns	NOs	Runs
60	54	4	952
Avg	50s	100s	Cts
19.04	4	-	12

Bowling

O	M	R	W
433.1	25	2,087	65
Avg	5WI	10WM	
32.11	1	—	

Highest score: 73 v MCC, Malahide 1996
Best bowling: 5-25 v Papua New Guinea, Ross Lord Park, Toronto 2001

In his third match, against MCC at Malahide, he came to the wicket with Ireland in trouble again on 127 for 5 and scored 73 out of a stand of 108 with Kyle McCallan, seeing his partner to his hundred.

In the second innings of that match he made 34 and took 3-32 and shortly afterwards against Sussex at Ormeau he took 4-66 with his brand of right-arm medium pace. Later that season he hit 45 against Scotland during the Triple Crown in Wales and 42 against Italy at the European Championships in Denmark but was less impressive with the ball. He suffered towards the latter part of the season with injury, primarily shin splints which cut his season short, but came back strong the following year and was selected by Ireland's first full-time national coach Mike Hendrick to travel to the ICC Trophy in Kuala Lumpur.

Heasley mostly batted at six or below for Ireland and could usually be relied upon to eke out a few runs late in an innings, particularly in the one-day form of the game where he was a fluent run-scorer who never threw his wicket away. He was a fearsome hitter of a ball, using his broad shoulders to good effect and giving wayward bowlers no place to hide.

Not selected for most of that ICC Trophy in KL, Heasley played in an easy ten-wicket win over Israel but then got a real chance to shine in the crucial semi-final against Kenya at Tenaga, where a victory would have qualified Ireland for the 1999 World Cup in England. He top scored that hot, sticky day with a courageous 51 off 48 balls as Ireland got to within seven runs of the Kenya total. A slow start by the Ireland top order meant that there was too much pressure on the players coming after and despite a fine rear-guard action by the likes of Heasley and a young Peter Gillespie (24 not out off 19 balls), the Irish fell agonisingly short of Kenya's modest total of 215.

Ireland also lost the final game of the tournament to Scotland and so the final qualification spot, with Heasley making 18 in a disappointing finale to what had been an encouraging ICC Trophy for Ireland.

Four years later was a different story, however, with the ICC Trophy in Canada marking the lowest point in the recent history of Irish cricket. As with most of the Irish team in that tournament, he failed to cover himself in glory despite taking career best figures of 5-25 in a nine-wicket win over Papua New Guinea at Ross Lord Park, Toronto.

Following the departure of then coach Ken Rutherford after the 2001 season, Heasley didn't last long under the new boss Adrian Birrell and retired from the Irish scene at the end of 2002 at the age of just thirty.

John Ganly Heaslip

RHB, OB; Dublin University, Leinster and Ireland (1920-33)

100 GREATS

Born: 26 November 1899, Dublin.
Died: 23 May 1966, Twickenham, London

Batting

Mts	Inns	NOs	Runs
18	30	2	720
Avg	50s	100s	Cts
25.71	4	-	8

Bowling

O	M	R	W
444	126	985	49
Avg	5WI	10WM	
20.10	3	-	

Highest score: 96 v Wales, Cardiff, 1923
Best bowling: 5-49 v MCC, College Park 1926

Jacko Heaslip was one of the best all-rounders in post-independence Ireland and his emigration to London at the end of the 1920s was a major blow.

He was educated at the King's Hospital school in Blackhall Place, where he first came to prominence as a sixteen-year-old in scoring 76 against High School. In 1917 he took 5-20 and made an unbeaten 118 against St Andrew's College. After captaining his school in 1918, he entered Trinity that June and became the star of a strong side.

A stylish and free-scoring batsman, he is still the only man to score more than 2,000 league runs for the university, reaching the thousand in 23 innings. In all games he made 3,211 runs in 103 innings – 992 in the summer of 1922, when he also took 44 wickets. That was the year he scored three of his five centuries for Trinity, 141, 139 and 126, as well as a 97 and 86 not out. His highest innings, 173 not out against Pembroke in 1921, came in two and a half hours.

He played for Leinster from the end of the student season in late June and totalled a record

780 league runs (average 43.30) in 1921, then beat it the following season with 889 (49.38), a record until professionals arrived in Leinster in the 1980s. He won the Marchant Cup for best batsman as well as the all-rounders trophy (he was runner-up all-rounder in 1921 and 1923).

He captained Trinity in 1923, when they finished third in the league and lost heavily to the West Indies in a low-scoring game, with Heaslip making 12 and 4. He played a handful of games in 1924 to little effect, although he made 100 against Manchester University.

He was first capped in 1920 as a replacement, one of seven debutants (five of whom were Trinity students) against Scotland in Edinburgh. This 'most gracious batsman' made his best score of 96 against Wales in Cardiff in 1923 and was left unbeaten with 92 against Scotland in 1927 when Ireland chased 175 to win but ended

two runs short. *The Irish Times* described it as 'one of the finest innings ever seen in College Park'. His best bowling performance came at College Park in 1926 when he took 4-41 and 5-49 against MCC.

He played a vital role in Ireland's most famous victory of the inter-war period, helping George McVeagh set a defendable target against the 1928 West Indians. Ireland led by 31 on first innings but were floundering on 88-5 when Heaslip went in. Soon it was 92-6 when he was joined by McVeagh and the pair set about repairing the innings. They put on 81 (Heaslip 44) before McVeagh, Thornton and Dixon took the total to 320. Ireland bowled the West Indies out for 291 and a 60-run victory.

In England he played for many years for Hounslow, and also for Civil Service and the Club Cricket Conference. He was awarded an OBE and died in London aged sixty-six.

100
GREATS

Conor Joseph Hoey

RHB, LB; CYM, Dublin University, Old Belvedere and Ireland (1991-95)

Conor Hoey was the best leg-spinner Ireland produced in the second half of the twentieth century but his career was shorter than it might have been in more sympathetic hands and with better luck with injuries.

He was the first cricketer to be capped out of the CYM club in Dublin, the brightest talent of a golden generation that also produced fast bowler Eddie Moore and several others who might have progressed had they stayed with the game.

Hoey made his senior debut for CYM aged fourteen, and was a fixture in South Leinster and international underage sides up to under-19s when he captained Ireland to third place behind two England sides in the annual tournament. Educated at Blackrock College, he went to UCD for a year before switching to Trinity where he was to break the club record for appearances (105) and wickets (221). While in Trinity he was

part of the second Irish University side to win the British Championship.

Hoey was picked to tour Zimbabwe in March 1991, and he won his first caps on that trip. He did well in the early tour games (recording what would be his best figures of 6-19 against a Mashonaland XI) but was murdered in the three-day game at Harare, with Alistair Campbell doing the greatest damage to his figures of 1-146. He was more than a match for another future Test captain later that year; when he bowled a juicy long hop to Brian Lara at Downpatrick he hit it straight to Mark Cohen at square leg. He was in fine form on the 1991 tour of England, taking 5-45 at Lord's and 6-82 v Wales at Usk.

A brisk leg-spinner, he pushed the ball through rather than rely on flight but the major drawback in his bowling was his inability to master the googly. At his peak in the early 1990s he was a novelty to county sides – one county

Born: Dublin, 24 March 1968

Batting

Mts	Inns	NOs	Runs
42	31	8	190
Avg	50s	100s	Cts
8.26	-	-	14

Bowling

O	M	R	W
696	128	2366	78
Avg	5WI	10WM	
30.33	4	-	

Highest innings: 34 v Middlesex, Castle Avenue 1992
Best bowling: 6-19 v Mashonaland Country Districts, Wedza, 1990-91

professional who played against him said 'That bloke's really good. He's twice as good as Ian Salisbury' (the leggie who played fifteen Tests with England).

A useful rugby player who won interprovincial honours, he developed shoulder problems. Despite operations and layoffs, the soreness persisted and meant an end to his international ambitions at just twenty-seven, an age when spin bowlers consider their best years to be ahead of them.

His last game was against Scotland in Rathmines shortly after Mike Hendrick took over in 1995. 'I was trying to build a career, I wasn't able to continue touring and giving so much time to playing for Ireland. Having started cricket at such an early age, the shoulder was sore, I wasn't bowling that well. It was more of a struggle to play than enjoyment.'

He bowled well at the 1994 ICC Trophy, when Ireland disappointingly missed out on World Cup qualification at the first attempt. Hoey twice won man of the match awards, for 10-2-29-5 against Papua New Guinea and 10-3-18-4 against Malaysia.

As a batsman he was impatient – and frequently irascible – but on the occasions he came off he could turn a match, including senior centuries for CYM and Trinity. He made an unbeaten 26 as Ireland fell short chasing a low Middlesex total in 1991, and 34 against the same side the following season. He took 601 wickets in Leinster senior cricket, 336 of them for CYM.

Leland Hone

RHB, WK; Dublin University, Phoenix, England and Ireland (1874-78)

Born: 30 January 1853, Dublin
Died: 31 December 1896, St Stephen's Green, Dublin

Batting

Mts	Inns	NOs	Runs	
11	19	2	332	
Avg	**50s**	**100s**	**Cts**	**Sts**
19.52	2	-	18	6

Highest innings: 74 not out v I Zingari, Phoenix CC 1877

Leland Hone is one of the rare group of Irishmen who played Test cricket, a distinction he achieved on the 1878-79 tour to Australia. At a late stage Lord Harris realised he was travelling without a wicketkeeper and Hone stepped into the breach. He played in the only Test match on that tour (it was only the third Test of all) and scored 7 and 6. He took two catches of Tom Emmett but allowed 19 byes. He was the first man to play for England without playing for a first-class county.

Hone was educated in England at Rugby School and entered Trinity College Dublin in January 1874. In his debut season he played for an XVIII of the university v the All England XI, making 0 and 7. He topped the bowling averages that year and the batting tables in 1876 with a high score of 47.

He was first picked for Ireland in 1874 for the visit of I Zingari, against whom he won six of his eleven caps. In his second game he made 16 and 47 and two years later made a free-hitting unbeaten 74. His batting was described as 'being of the flashing order'. *The Irish Times* obituary said that 'his freedom of style was refreshing to watch'.

He made a couple of unsuccessful appearances for MCC against Oxford and Cambridge in neither game keeping wicket – but was soon behind the stumps for Lord Harris's tourists. His best contribution with the bat (he always went in No.11) was 24.

He toured again in May 1879, this time with Ireland on a short foray to London. Hone made 6 against MCC at Lord's and 4 against Surrey. On a similar trip four years later he made 25★ v MCC and 72 against the Aldershot Division. He kept wicket in six of his eleven caps, holding twelve catches elsewhere in the field.

Hone was part of one of the great cricket dynasties, with two of his brothers, three of his cousins and his nephew all playing for Ireland. In September 1879 Leland went to America with the Irish team captained by his brother Nat, but missed the capped matches. Leland suffered in later years from heart disease and died suddenly at home in St Stephen's Green, aged forty-three, having been walking around Dublin that morning. He is buried in Mount Jerome cemetery.

RHB, SLA; City of Derry, Eglinton and Ireland (1951-66)

Born: 21 December 1923, Ture, County Donegal

Batting

Mts	Inns	NOs	Runs
36	48	9218	5.59
Avg	50s	100s	Cts
-	-	-	22

Bowling

O	M	R	W
942.5	293	2314	112
Avg	5WI	10WM	
20.66	7	1	

Highest innings: 23 not out v MCC, College Park 1954

Best bowling: 8-48 v MCC, College Park, 1954

Scott Huey was the first native North-Westerner to make a big impact for Ireland, and his quality left-arm spin was a vital feature of Irish sides of his time. North-West wicketkeeper Shaun Bradley paid him this tribute: 'The best bowler I ever kept to was Scott Huey, who was also a great motivator and played with passion.'

Huey was educated at the Masonic School in Dublin and made his senior debut for City of Derry aged twenty. In the fourth game of that season he took 5-13 against Donemana and won his first league medal in 1946. He moved to Eglinton in 1948 where he joined a strong side featuring LC Head, Bobby Taylor and Tommy Orr, and proved to be the final piece in a jigsaw of what became one of the strongest North-West teams of all. His move paid early dividends in that year's senior cup final when he came after Brigade were set 123 to win. Huey took a hat-trick and 7-41 to give Eglinton the cup.

The following year he was 'unplayable' in taking all 10 for 10 against Donemana who, chasing

52, were bowled out for 20. Davy Todd recalled him 'Bowling left arm round to right-hand batsmen, coming in behind the umpire.' His feats started to attract attention further afield and he was eventually picked for Ulster and, in 1951, for Ireland. The first of his thirty-five caps came against Scotland when he took five wickets in the match in tandem with Jimmy Boucher, who took eight.

He took 4-83 against India at Ormeau but was kept out of the Irish side for two years by Jack Bowden and Sonny Hool. He was recalled in September 1954 for the visit of MCC to College Park. He took 6-49 in the first innings but MCC looked set for an easy win with just 155 for victory in the fourth innings. With his immaculate command of length and a lethal faster delivery, Huey ran through a side containing three England captains, with his 8-48 ensuring a two-run win. His match return of 14-97 raced him to the top of English first-class averages for that year with 6.92 and there he remains for ever more. There was never another day like that, of course, but Huey had several more starring performances, often against professional sides. He took 5-46 against the 1957 West Indies, 7-84 against Lancashire in 1959, and 5-68 against the 1965 New Zealanders.

He continued to star in local cricket, taking 9-9 against City of Derry and 10-28 v Donemana. He bowled unchanged for five hours in the 1958 cup semi-final against Donemana, taking 9-67 in a losing cause. His efforts helped Eglinton to the treble in 1956 and when he finally retired in 1973 he had two league medals, five cups and six Faughan Valley cups. He also played badminton for Ireland and hockey for Ulster.

He was also a superb captain and even aged forty-three was the obvious choice for the North-West side in the first Guinness Cup interprovincial series in 1966. He took 15 wickets at less than ten and his canny leadership saw the union to the title, which they repeated in 1969. From 1966-71 he took 68 wickets at 10.69 – still the leading average – in twenty-four interprovincial appearances. He was later a selector for Ireland.

One of his proudest moments was captaining Ireland – which he did five times in all – at Beechgrove in 1963, the first international to be played in the city. In the fourth innings Scotland were 114-4 chasing 201 when Huey struck. They were all out for 131 as Huey returned figures of 16-11-13-6. He also rates a footnote in the history of first-class as the last man to dismiss Len Hutton (for 89, stumped by Colhoun, in College Park, 1960).

There is much debate in the North-West over the relative merits of Huey and John Flood, Sion Mills's slow left armer, although the figures come down comprehensively on the side of Huey. The pair were big box-office hits and their rivalry persisted for two decades, although the modest Huey always refrained from commenting on the matter.

100 GREATS

John William Hynes

RHB/LB; Dublin University, Phoenix. Leinster and Ireland (1883-1896)

Jack Hynes was an outstanding schoolboy cricketer at Clongowes, who entered Trinity in May 1883 and went straight into the first XI, where he remained for seven years. The dominant personality of the 1880s, he still holds the highest partnership for the ninth wicket for Ireland and the ground record for College Park.

He was barely in the gates of Trinity when he scored 115 against Civil Service, the first of his ten centuries for college sides. He was rapidly elevated to the Ireland side, and made 19 and 18 at Lord's that July. Retained for the visit of I Zingari, he made a belligerent 46 and took 4-46 in a losing cause. He was an automatic choice for the next decade, although he was only twice named captain – earning a win and a draw despite losing both tosses.

The Philadelphians toured in 1884, and the *American Cricketer* reported that Hynes was 'The Champion Bat of Ireland' after scoring 41 and 58 for Dublin University.

With WD Hamilton he set a record ninth-wicket stand of 96 against Canada in Rathmines in 1887, a mark equalled by Davy Dennison and Mike Halliday ninety-nine years later.

Hynes organised the 1888 tour to North America but was pipped for the captaincy by one vote in a contest with Dominic Cronin. The affront certainly did not affect his performances, as he ended the tour as leading bowler and his batting was second only to John Dunn. In the major matches he made 62 against Canada and 72 ('a fine innings') against Philadelphia, totalling 500 runs at an average of 28. He also took 78 wickets at just over seven, his 6-17 v Canada at Toronto being the match-winning performance. In a minor game against Ottawa he scored 61 and took 10-12.

Born: 1864
Died: 16 July 1930.

Batting

Mts	Inns	NOs	Runs
29	43	3	937
Avg	50s	100s	Cts
23.42	5	-	20

Bowling

O	M	R	W
359.2	107	779	63
Avg	5WI	10WM	
12.36	5	1	

Highest score: 97 v WH Laverton's XI, Westbury 1893
Best bowling: 6-17 v Canada, Toronto 1888

He and Jack Meldon were the only tourists to return in 1892, when Hynes took 5-23 and 3-50 to record a rare Irish win over Philadelphia on American soil. He made his two highest scores for Ireland in the space of four days on the English tour of 1893, 91 against Combined Services was followed by 97 against WH Laverton's XI.

For Trinity he was a free-scoring opener, rattling up 3,022 runs in his seven years on the XI, with a best of 589 at 58.9 in 1888. He also took 233 wickets, including 58 at 8.6 in 1887, the second of his two years as captain. His biggest innings was an unbeaten 241 made against the Dublin Garrison in May 1888, although *The Irish Times* was not convinced of its merits after the first day: 'Mr Hynes was not out with 208 to his credit. He only gave one chance – a hot return to the bowler just after he completed his second century. However the wretched bowling and fielding of the visitors detracted somewhat from the merit of the innings which was chiefly remarkable for fine all-round hitting'. Play continued in the morning but was abandoned due to rain with Trinity on 370-5. He also made 230* v Bangor in 1884.

Hynes worked as a barrister and was appointed a county court judge in Cork in 1916.

Born: 14 August 1910, Dublin
Died: 13 March 1973, Basingstoke, Hampshire

Batting

Mts	Inns	NOs	Runs
48	84	3	1628
Avg	50s	100s	Cts
20.10	10	-	21

Bowling

O	M	R	W
1393	513	3038	151
Avg	5WI	10WM	
20.12	7	1	

Highest Innings: 83 v MCC, Lord's 1935
Best bowling: 7-83 v Australians, College Park 1938

In an interview published shortly before his death, Eddie Ingram said 'I always played cricket as a hobby. It was my major interest. I enjoyed every minute of my long innings.' And his innings proved as successful as it was long.

Ingram joined the Leinster club in 1920, aged ten, and was first capped as a schoolboy in Belvedere College, for whom he and Jimmy Boucher were a dominant force. On his Irish debut he didn't bowl and batted at No.8, but innings of 11 and 14* showed promise.

He had a very resolute defence, strong off the back foot and on the leg side, a savage puller and hooker of anything bowled short of a length. He was very fast between the wickets. In a celebrated incident against MCC at Rathmines, he ran four and wanted a fifth but his partner pleaded 'For Christ's sake no more Chicken, I'm shagged'. As a bowler he delivered leg-breaks but later turned to slow in-swing.

His club record was astonishing: From the age of eighteen to twenty-four – when he left Dublin for London – no one could take the LCU all-rounder trophy off him. He was the only man to take 14 wickets (6-40, 8-63 against Phoenix in 1931) during the era when some, usually bank holiday, league games were played over two innings. He took ten in a match on four occasions. He won the batting cup in 1932 with an average of 73 and again in 1933 when he had a run of 103*, 100*, 64, 213, 86, 85. In 1933 he made 213 out of 506-9 against Phoenix; 'he cut their strong attack to shreds' recalled Paddy Boland, who also noted that he was 'supremely shrewd at finding out the strengths and weaknesses of opponents – and teammates'.

Ingram made nine senior centuries and 21 fifties for Leinster. He only played eighty-three competitive games for the club but scored 3,416 runs at 46.16 (behind only Bray, Botha and Masood) and took 325 wickets at 9.13 (second only to O'Riordan).

According to DR Pigot senior, Ingram was 'one of the steadiest bowlers imaginable. Under conditions that suited him he was almost unplayable, and at any time could make the best of batsmen fight for their runs. He bowled with a small amount of break but relied on slow deceptive flight and immaculate length. He was a very defensive bowler unless conditions suited.'

Ingram won forty-eight Irish caps and was captain on eight occasions. Among his many tremendous performances several stand out. He had two brilliant innings of 78 and 83 at Lord's in 1935 but when the 1938 Australians arrived in College Park in end-of-term mood they were rattled to be bowled out by Ireland for 145, with Ingram taking 7-83. In 1949 Yorkshire were cruising at 286-5 when Ingram came on – and collapsed to 293 all out (Ingram 5-0).

He had some fine displays against Sir Julian Cahn's XI, notably in 1938 when Ireland won by an innings against a side that included Test players Dempster, Morkel and Crisp. Ingram bowled 54 overs in the match taking 10-73 in tandem with Boucher (7-88).

His career at Guinness saw him transferred to Park Royal brewery in 1936 (having just won his eighth league title in succession with Leinster), and joined the Ealing club in London. *Wisden* recorded that 'he took over 3,000 wickets for them with varied bowling of impeccable length besides regularly scoring 1,000 runs a season'. The primrose annual also described him as 'a great character of Pickwickian girth'.

He played a dozen games for Middlesex before and after the war, captaining the side on occasion. He took a wicket, that of Syd Buller, with his second ball for the county. According to Pat Hone, 'It was the opinion at Lord's that if they had got him earlier, and taught him to bowl more antagonistically, considerable honours in English cricket would have come his way'.

He got a few chances to the show his skills, particularly in wartime festival games, as *Wisden* described in 1941: 'The British Empire Team beat a Yorkshire Eleven containing nine county players by four wickets... that clever Irish and Middlesex bowler, E A Ingram, took 6-26.' He also played for the Club Cricket Conference against the 1947 South Africans.

Thomas Ormsby Jameson
RHB, RF/LBG; Phoenix, Hampshire and Ireland (1926-28)

100 GREATS

Tommy Jameson was a gentleman amateur who played twice for Ireland and would have played much more had he not been a career soldier who also played for Hampshire.

His debut came in 1926 at The Parks, when he watched from the far end as Ireland collapsed from 97-1 to 221 all out, his own contribution being a top-scoring 71. The game was ruined by weather, but Jameson claimed 4-140. His last cap came two years later in the famous victory over the West Indies at College Park, when he top-scored in the first innings with 45*,

described by his captain Jim Ganly as 'a very fine innings'. He helped bowl Ireland to a first innings lead with 11.2-4-17-3. He was bowled for 5 second time around and chipped in with 2-75 as the Windies fell 60 runs short.

He learned the game at Harrow, and played in the most famous of all school games, the celebrated 'Fowler's Match' which saw an incredible performance for Eton by the County Meath-born Bob Fowler. With 54 to win, Jameson opened the batting and spent an hour on 0. He was ninth man out for 2, with the score on 32.

Born: 4 April 1892, Clonsilla, Co. Dublin
Died: 6 February 1965, Dun Laoghaire, Co. Dublin

Batting

Mts	Inns	NOs	Runs
2	3	1	121
Avg	50s	100s	Cts
60.50	1	-	3

Bowling

O	M	R	W
78.2	19	232	9
Avg	5WI	10WM	
25.78	-	-	

Highest innings: 71 v Oxford University, The Parks, 1926
Best bowling: 4-140 v Oxford University, The Parks, 1926

As a schoolboy home from England he often played alongside Fowler on Na Shuler tours. Pat Hone recalled that 'As a youth he was a fastish bowler of rather 'help yourself' stuff, but when he took to bowling slow leg-breaks, it was a very different story.' He played for Phoenix before joining up in 1914. He remained in the army at the end of the war, turning out for Hampshire and services sides whenever he could. He was a keen rackets player and was squash champion of England on two occasions.

One contemporary wrote that 'His free and stylish batting was always a pleasure to see,' and he was good enough to make five first-class centuries, including 103 batting at number 8 v Warwickshire in 1925. In 124 first-class games he made 4,675 runs at 26.56, with a highest score of 133 made for SB Joel's XI against Orange Free State in Bloemfontein in 1924/25. That side was very strong and there was much debate concerning whether the games against South Africa would rank as Tests, but as England were touring Australia at the time it was rejected. Jameson finished second in the averages on that tour with 430 runs at 39 including 53* in the 'Test' that wasn't.

Jameson was able to tour several times with MCC, visiting West Indies in 1925/26 (98 v West Indies and 110 v Jamaica) and South America in 1926/27 (centuries in Uruguay and Argentina). In 1937/38 he went to India with Lord Tennyson's side but played just six games and never shone.

As a bowler he took 252 first-class wickets at 24.04 with a best of 7-92 – including Ernest Tyldesley and Charlie Hallows – against Lancashire in 1925 A teammate at Hampshire, HLV Day, wrote about Jameson in *Wisden*: 'T O Jameson… was a regular soldier and his opportunities were strictly limited. But whenever he played, or rather was allowed to bowl before batsmen had got dug in, Jameson always looked likely to get wickets. He bowled slow right-arm from an enormous height, he stood six feet four, which appeared absolute jam from the ringside but had even the best batsmen in a bother. He was not merely a technically perfect bowler, he was a schemer, constantly probing a batsman's weakness, or playing upon his indulgence. In addition, he became a very stylish batsman with immense wristy power as befitted an amateur rackets champion. A great pity he could not play more frequently.'

He died in a Dun Laoghaire hospital in 1965.

Paul Barry Jackson

WK, RHB; North of Ireland and Ireland (1981-94)

Born: 9 December 1959, Belfast

Batting

Mts	Inns	NOs	Runs	
87	86	18	987	
Avg	50s	100s	Cts	Sts
14.51	2	–	103	30

Bowling

O	M	R	W
1.2	-	6	1
Avg	5WI	10WM	
6.00	-	-	

Highest score: 89 not out v Wales, Welshpool 1987

Best bowling: 1-2 v Mashonland, Norton 1986

If it wasn't for the presence of North-West legend Ossie Colhoun there would be no doubt that Paul Jackson was Ireland's best wicketkeeper to date. Even as it stands there are still plenty of people quick to give him that label.

'I would put Paul Jackson in the one-of-the-best-wicketkeepers-I've-ever-seen category from any country,' said former Ireland team-mate and winner of 121 caps, Alan Lewis. 'He had an ability to stop even genuine leg glances and standing back I never saw a better keeper. He was way, way up there with the best. Top drawer,' he said.

Jackson was never the most tidily dressed keeper with bits of trouser sticking out from behind patched-up pads, his cap jauntily askew and shirt tails hanging but he was pristine when it came to his positioning and glove-work. In August 1990 he spent 123 overs behind the sticks in the first innings against Scotland in Edinburgh without conceding one bye. And this was not unusual. In fact it was more noteworthy

on days when he did let one sneak through, even if it should really have been called a wide.

Statistically he was the second most successful keeper Ireland produced, taking 103 catches and 30 stumpings in eighty-seven appearances. While Colhoun took 148 catches and 42 stumpings in the same number of caps, it should be pointed out that Jackson played more one-day cricket than his predecessor so he had less time in the middle to catch up. Jackson holds the record for the most catches in an innings with six against Scotland at Titwood, Glasgow in 1984, a feat equalled by Niall O'Brien during a 2006 European Championship match against Italy.

There was always something going on with Jackson in the side. He was an effective if not an altogether orthodox batsman and was certainly a more useful all-round player than the great Colhoun. He had one shot that his teammates dubbed the 'revolving door' where he would take a ball anywhere from two feet outside the

off-stump and hit it backward of square leg by almost turning a complete circle.

Although he never scored a century for Ireland, he did manage an 89 not out against Wales at Welshpool in 1987. That game was another where he remained byeless while also managing to captain Ireland.

In all he led the country on twenty-five occasions but only had one victory and eight draws to show for it, a fairly ordinary record, even by Irish standards. Of course, he did not have the sort of quality players with him that some of his predecessors such as Mike Halliday and Dermott Monteith enjoyed.

'Paul was a magnificent keeper and a superb team player,' said former teammate John Elder. 'To go on a tour with Jacko was a treat, he was the very best of company and watching him keep wicket was a joy. Standing back he cut everything off and standing up the ball invariably stuck in his gloves. He would be an automatic choice in my top Irish team,' said Elder.

RHB, RMF, Dublin University, Transvaal, South Africa and Ireland (1890-93)

Born: 31 March 1871, Carbury, County Kildare
Died: 31 May 1908, Maraisburg, Roodepoort, Transvaal, South Africa

Batting

Mts	Inns	NOs	HS	Runs
12	17	1	76	330
Avg	50s	100s	Cts	
20.63	2	-	13	

Bowling

O	M	R	W
271.2	100	537	3236
Avg	Best	5WI	
14.91	5-23	1	

Highest innings: 76 v I Zingari, Vice-Regal Ground, 1892
Best bowling: 5-23 v I Zingari, Vice-Regal Ground, 1892

Clem 'Boy' Johnson is one of the small group of Irish-born cricketers to play the game at Test-match level. Johnson's moment of glory came on 2 March 1896 at Johannesburg, when he lined up for South Africa alongside fellow Irishman Reggie Poore. Dubliner Sir Timothy O'Brien played for England in the same game. Johnson made 7 and 3 and had figures of 28-12-57-0 in what was his only Test.

Johnson was educated at the Royal Naval College in London, where he was in the XI from 1886-88 when he entered Trinity College Dublin. Six foot tall, he was a fast right-arm bowler and a good fielder. He was described by *Cricket: A Weekly Record of the Game* as being a 'useful batsman with sound methods'.

He went straight onto the first XI at Trinity and topped the bowling averages in his first season with 36 wickets at 12.3. Over five seasons he took 207 wickets. He was a useful batsman against top opposition, making 28 and 21 against Arthur Shrewsbury's XI in 1891 and 49 and 56 v Cambridge University (whose bowlers included future Test bowlers Stanley Jackson and Hugh Bromley-Davenport) in 1892. He took 4-2 for Trinity in a remarkable win over Warwickshire when the county were bowled out for 15.

Johnson was first picked for Ireland against Scotland in 1890, scoring 20 and 7 and taking 2-102. He went on tour to North America in the autumn of 1892, but his performances were poor, perhaps affected by an incident on the journey across when he was almost swept overboard in a storm.

His best performances for Ireland came earlier that summer against I Zingari when he made his best score of 76 and best bowling on 11.2-1-23-5. He picked up wickets steadily and economically but never ran through a side again. His batting was disappointing for Ireland, with a string of low scores before he made 36, 0, 46 and 71 on the tour of England in 1893, which was his farewell to Irish cricket.

Suffering from ill health he emigrated to the Transvaal. He returned to the northern hemisphere within six months, however, as part of the first South Africa touring party after a couple of good innings – including 52 v Eastern Province – for his newly-adopted state. The tour was a financial disaster and a wet summer meant the conditions were alien to many of the party. Johnson scored 508 runs at 14.32 and took 50 wickets (17.27). He made 112 against Liverpool & District and took 6-41 against Warwickshire. The Irish leg of the tour was successful for Johnson, making 79 against Ireland 'in brilliant style', and he also took 3-0 with the ball. Against Trinity he took 3-28 and 6-33.

He later played for the Wanderers club in Johannesburg, and his final first-class game was against Lord Hawke's tourists in 1898-99. He died suddenly in Roodeport aged just thirty-seven.

100 GREATS

David Trent Johnston
RAF, RHB; Carlisle, Clontarf, New South Wales and Ireland (2004-)

One of five players on this list who originally came to Ireland as overseas club professionals (the others being Charles Lawrence, Jeremy Bray, Raman Lamba and Andre Botha), Trent Johnston first came with a fine reputation from Sydney in 1995 to play for the now defunct Carlisle club in south Dublin.

For several years he would return to the antipodes in winter and he was selected to play Sheffield Shield cricket for New South Wales in the 1998-99 and 1999-2000 seasons on the strength of being the leading wicket-taker in grade cricket for two seasons running. A strapping right-arm fast bowler and quick-scoring, hard-hitting middle-order batsman, Johnston never really established himself as an integral part of the NSW team but was a formidable force in Grade 1 for his clubs Mosman, North Sydney and Campbelltown. In October 2003, he took a hat-trick against University of New South Wales, including the wicket of 74-Test veteran batsman Michael Slater.

But by that stage, Johnston's future was in Ireland where he lives full-time with his Irish wife and two children and plays for the Clontarf club. He made his debut for his adopted country in 2004 as they beat Surrey by four wickets in the C&G Trophy at Castle Avenue and although he never displayed the sort of out-and-out pace that he did as a younger bowler, he quickly established himself as a consistent performer who could be relied upon to bowl tight lines under pressure.

He took seven wickets on a batsman's track in the ICC Intercontinental Cup semi-final against the United Arab Emirates in Windhoek, including 5-33 in the first innings. Unfortunately in the final against Kenya he broke a finger while fielding and despite doing his best to continue, he was unable to bowl again in the match.

A pivotal part of the Irish middle-order, Johnston's contributions batting at six or seven have been invaluable.

He hit 67 in good support of centurion Ed Joyce to ensure victory over the UAE in the ICC Trophy at Stormont in 2005 and made another crucial 44 in the winning semi-final against Canada in Clontarf. A powerful straight hitter, there are few grounds that have a long

David Trent Johnston
continued

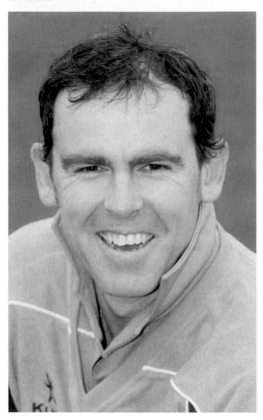

Born: 29 April 1974, Woollongong, New South Wales

Batting

Mts	Inns	NOs	Runs
36	35	4	747
Avg	50s	100s	Cts
24.10	5	-	16

Bowling

O	M	R	W
339.2	52	1,371	61
Avg	5WI	10WM	
22.48	2	-	

Highest score: 83 v Denmark, Utrecht 2004

Best bowling: 6-23 v Namibia, Castle Avenue 2006

enough boundary to worry Johnston when he gets his eye in and he has the ability to change the complexion of an innings in a few short overs.

His best innings for Ireland so far was probably the 83 he scored off 70 balls against Denmark in the 2004 European Championships in Utrecht. Coming in with his side in a bit of trouble at 85 for 4, he and former captain Kyle McCallan put on 140 for the fifth wicket in a cultured partnership that was devoid of undue risks but that had the fluency of scoring at more than a run a ball in what were difficult batting conditions. It showed Johnston as more than just a big hitter, a batsman capable of building an ultimately match-winning innings in trying circumstances.

He was made captain at the end of the summer of 2005, taking over from Ireland's most-capped skipper Jason Molins, and he rapidly established his own style of leadership. A passionate and thoughtful captain, Johnston leads from the front, taking the responsibility of bringing himself on to bowl at crucial stages of games. A natural competitor, he backs himself to deliver and manages successfully to instil that belief in the rest of the squad. He can also be found leading the sing-song after successful matches. His rendition of 'Singing In The Rain' is fast acquiring legendary status.

Dominick Ignatius Joyce

RHB, RAM; Merrion, Dublin University and Ireland (2000-)

Born: 14 June 1981, Dublin

Bating

Mts	Inns	NOs	Runs
62	63	4	1,435
Avg	50s	100s	Cts
24.32	11	–	12

Bowling

O	M	R	W
20	2	64	1
Avg	5WI	10WM	
64.00	-	-	

Highest score: 67 v Wiltshire, South Wiltshire 2001

Best bowling: 1-26 v Netherlands, Deventer 2004

One of five Joyce siblings to have played cricket for Ireland, Dominick emerged from the shadow of his elder brother Ed with a number of vital innings for his country. His other brother Gus won three international caps in a cricket career dogged by injury, Ed played fifty times before selection for England A and later the full England one-day side in 2006 rendered him ineligible, and his younger sisters, twins Cecelia and Isobel, remain a central part of the Irish women's team.

Although the youngest boy in the family, Dominick is now the most-capped Joyce and while he has struggled with his consistency, particularly when opening the batting, he is a gutsy player with shots all around the wagon wheel. He is a crisp driver of the ball, relishing anything full of a length and he is not afraid to take on the short ball either side of the wicket.

'He has been quite flexible in the batting order, probably to his own detriment,' said national coach Adrian Birrell. 'Early season wickets or those with plenty of lateral movement don't really suit him. For that reason, I think he would be a much better player out of the country on harder, truer wickets than in Ireland,' he said.

That said, the 31 and 61 he scored against Scotland in a low-scoring ICC Intercontinental Cup match in Aberdeen in 2005 is perhaps his finest hour so far. On a green-top wicket inappropriate considering the match's first-class status, Joyce battled hard in both innings at number four and set Ireland a total that they just managed to defend, winning the match by three runs.

But his failure to register big scores at the top of the innings has meant his place in the side has never been 100 per cent assured. A ratio of one to six, half-centuries to innings, is more than respectable but his failure to go on to the magic three figures and beyond has cost him. Indeed, his tendency to get out between 50 and 65 is holding him back but with a long way to go in his playing career there is still time to rectify the situation.

The second highest-capped Dublin University player behind Michael Halliday and the most-capped for Merrion, he represented Ireland at various underage levels, playing in the ICC U19 World Cup in Sri Lanka in 2000.

Edmund Christopher Joyce

LHB, RAM; Merrion, Dublin University and Ireland (1997-2005)

100 GREATS

Born: 22 September 1978, Dublin

Batting

Mts	Inns	NOs	Runs
50	51	7	1,637
Avg	50s	100s	Cts
37.20	12	2	19

Bowling

O	M	R	W
67.4	2	360	7
Avg	5WI	10WM	
51.43	-	-	

Highest score: 115 not out v United Arab Emirates, Stormont 2005
Best bowling: 2-27 v Earl of Arundel's XI, Arundel Castle 1997

From a very early age Ed Joyce showed signs of having something special. As a small-for-his-age teenager, he played in the men's junior leagues for his club Merrion CC and regularly scored heavily against players twice his age and three times his size. It was clear from a very early stage that Joyce was going to be a star.

Joyce comes from one of Ireland's great cricketing families, two of his four brothers – Dominick and Augustine – have represented Ireland at senior level. Dom is represented here while Gus perhaps would have been but for recurring injuries that limited his international career to just three caps and prematurely ended his club cricket days.

Also in the family, Joyce's younger sisters, twins Cecelia and Isobel, are mainstays of the Ireland women's cricket team and have been since they were teenagers.

But Ed is undoubtedly the most successful of the family and he also has the drive, determination and desire required to be successful at the highest level of sport.

Having established himself on Merrion's first team by the age of sixteen, Joyce was selected on various representative sides at underage level, scoring centuries at schools and under-19 levels. He also played for Dublin University when the time came but not before he had made his full international debut in 1997, against Scotland at the age of eighteen, scoring a high-class 60. It was then that he was offered a trial with Middlesex.

'I played one game (for the second team), didn't do particularly well, didn't enjoy it and didn't play again until two years later,' he said. 'I didn't get a good vibe off it. I didn't really think I was good enough. I didn't think the guys were very nice at the time and the atmosphere wasn't great at Middlesex. They weren't doing very well.

'But they kept badgering me so two years later I just said I might as well shut them up by going back over. And I did well.' That was 1999 and in that time a new generation of young Middlesex cricketers, with Joyce at the forefront, helped turn the county's fortunes around.

Because of his commitment to Middlesex and his desire to play for England, Joyce's Ireland career was effectively over before its time. Of his fifty caps, forty-five of them came before the end of 2001. He was brought back for the 2005 ICC Trophy in Ireland and helped his country qualify for the 2007 World Cup finals with five innings of real quality. He scored 103, 40, 115 not out, 60 and 81, averaging almost 100, as Ireland made it through to the final and a place in the West Indies was theirs. His innings against the United Arab Emirates was perhaps his most impressive in Irish colours and not just because it was his highest. At the wicket with Ireland struggling on 23 for 4 chasing 231 for victory, Joyce put on 122 for the fifth wicket with Trent Johnston and then saw the side home with just the tail for company, manipulating the strike and controlling the game under high-pressure circumstances. Ireland finally won with one ball and two wickets to spare with Joyce unbeaten on 115.

At his best, Joyce is the sort of player who can score at a run a ball without anyone realising.

A left-hander with a silky cover drive, he has the knack of hitting gaps for singles off decent balls while also being able to despatch the bad ones to the boundary. In 2006 he turned his talents on his own when he hit a savage 95 for Middlesex against Ireland in the C&G Trophy at Lord's. He was finally out, short of his century having faced just 73 balls, showing that while not renowned as a destructive batsman, on his day he can make good bowlers grovel.

Not surprisingly, once Joyce had satisfied a four-year residency criterion to make himself eligible for England, he soon attracted the attentions of the selectors. He was picked for the England Academy squad for the winter of 2005 and then toured with England A to the West Indies early in 2006. He made his full one-day international debut for England, ironically against Ireland in June 2006, in the first ever match between the two countries. Unlike a few weeks previously when playing for Middlesex, he did not perform with the bat that day at Stormont, making just ten before giving up a catch to midwicket.

In his second appearance for England, a Twenty20 match against Sri Lanka at the Rose Bowl, Joyce suffered a nasty injury to his ankle that put him out of contention just when he looked like breaking into the team. His England career remains in the balance but his place in the heart of the Middlesex middle order looks assured.

While his overall batting average for Ireland is more than respectable at 37.2, it would be fair to say that had he continued to play for the country of his birth he could have expected it to rise further. In his last 13 innings for Ireland he scored more than 750 runs at an average of 75.8 and in all first-class cricket he is averaging nearly 47.

'It became very clear, very quickly that he had something that the rest of us just didn't have,' said former Ireland teammate Kyle McCallan. 'He just had any amount of time and the ability to play all the shots in the book. He is the best batsman that I have ever played with on the Irish side, the most all-round complete batsman,' he said.

While Joyce now has his eyes set firmly on wearing the three lions of England on his chest rather than the shamrock of Ireland, he remains arguably the finest batsman this country has ever produced and certainly the best of his generation. How far his talent will take him in the game over the coming years remains to be seen.

Augustine Patrick Kelly

RHB, WK; Phoenix, Dublin University and Ireland (1920-30)

A P Kelly was one of the outstanding personalities of the 1920s, a batsman who relished a challenge and never flinched against the fastest bowling. A teammate summed him up as 'Never a fair-weather cricketer and at his own queer best in adversity.'

He was educated at the Jesuit college of Ampleforth in Yorkshire before entering Trinity in June 1912. He played two seasons on the first XI before the Great War, making 465 runs at 27 in 1914, when he took over as wicketkeeper.

After the war he returned to complete his degree and took over as captain for the debut season of the Leinster Senior League and made 628 runs at 24.1. He made his only century for Trinity in 1920, 143 against the Dover Garrison, with 897 runs at 38.88 in a prolific season. He topped the LCU wicketkeeping rankings each season from 1919-21.

According to Pat Hone, Kelly was 'something of a martinet' in his role as captain, being fond of inspecting the team's boots to ensure they were properly spiked. Kelly was captain of Lord's in

Born: 1894, Dublin, Ireland
Died: 12 May 1960, Hackney, London

Batting

Mts	Inns	NOs	Runs	Avg
25	41	2	810	20.76
50s	100s	Cts	Sts	
4	-	27	14	

Bowling

O	M	R	W	Avg
2	0	6	0	-

Highest score: 82 v Wales, Cardiff 1923

1929 when George McVeagh turned up late in borrowed flannels and tennis shoes, explaining that his taxi had been in a collision and that he had left his cricket bag in the car. Kelly received the news in chilly fashion and told the rest of the team that for the rest of the game they were not to talk to McVeagh, who was also relegated to No.8 in the order.

He made his debut in the first game after the First World War, and made his highest score against Wales in 1923. He made only 4 fifties, but several other smaller scores were crucial innings.

His former teammate DR Pigot senior said of him 'At his best Kelly was a very high-class keeper and bat. Perhaps his finest asset was his "gutfulness" in dealing with unpleasant fast bowling of which Irish cricketers get little exposure.' Pigot went on the tell a story of the 1924 West Indians game against a Trinity Past & Present XI. Kelly had taken 'a bang or two' in the first innings from George Francis, the West Indies tearaway quickie. 'As he buckled on his pads in the pavilion to open the second innings he remarked to his companion 'I'll teach that black d------ to bowl at me'. He duly hit 14 or 16 off the first over from Francis.'

There are several more tales of his cussedness on and off the field. At Chelmsford in 1922, he came in with Trinity at 0-2 against Essex, and made 98 to save the game.

He was skilful too, however, and when Trinity played Cambridge in 1920 the locals were confounded by a 'gluey' track. Kelly was first in, last out, making 65 against bowlers such as future Test leg-spinner CS Marriott and just failing to save the match. Pigot wrote in 1941: 'I can still vividly remember a hundred Kelly made in 1921 against Kent Club and Ground at Maidstone against two fast bowlers on a damaged wicket when most of us were worrying about our heads rather than our wickets.'

Gustavus William Francis Blake Kelly

RHB, RF; Co. Galway, Oxford University and Ireland (1895-1914)

Born: 2 April 1877, Dublin
Died: 16 August 1951, Dundermott, Ballymoe, County Roscommon

Batting

Mts	Inns	NOs	Runs
19	30	6	280
Avg	**50s**	**100s**	**Cts**
11.66	-	-	9

Bowling

O	M	R	W
275.2	61	788	53
Avg	**5WI**	**10WM**	
14.86	2	1	

Highest score: 40* v I Zingari, Vice Regal 1906
Best bowling: 8-30 v I Zingari, Vice Regal 1906

Gus Kelly was a tall fast bowler who was one of the most important figures of the Golden Age in Irish cricket. Although he only played nineteen games, they were spread over twenty summers and he left a lasting legacy to the game through his two sons who were also capped.

He had a peripatetic childhood, attending school at Clongowes Wood in Ireland and Oratory School, Windsor College, Beaumont College and Stonyhurst in England. He went up to Lincoln College, Oxford, in 1898 and represented the university at golf, cricket and athletics, winning the long jump at the inter-varsities meeting. He won his cricket blue in 1901 and 1902, making few runs in either game, although he took 3-19 and 2-51 in a losing cause in the second year. He took 28 wickets at 27 and scored 448 runs at almost 20, with one fifty.

His first games for Ireland were on the English tour in 1895, but he was a peripheral figure in all three matches. He didn't play again

until 1901 but little should be read into this as Ireland only played three games in that time.

The South Africans came to Dublin in 1901, and after a middle order collapse Kelly 'restored the situation, making some hefty swipes' in making 30. He took four wickets against London County at the Mardyke in 1903, including that of WG Grace, caught by Kelly's brother-in-law Dan Comyn. Cambridge University was beaten by an innings the following year, with Kelly claiming 3-32 in the second innings.

He had several other excellent returns for Ireland, notably 3-9 against Yorkshire in 1907 and 4-62 against the county the following summer. He took 8-30 and 4-56 v I Zingari in the last international played at the Vice-Regal Lodge in 1906, and 8-60 in the match against the Scots in College Park in 1910.

Two of his sons, Gus and Achey, also won Irish caps. His elder son, GN, was 'strongly reminiscent of his father' according to Pat Hone: he was tall, loosely built, a swift bowler and big hitter.

Francis Greetham Kempster
RHB, RM; Co Galway, Dublin University, Leinster and Ireland (1874-77)

Born: 5 October 1853
Died: 21 November 1934

Batting

Mts	Inns	NOs	Runs
3	8	1	195
Avg	50s	100s	Cts
21.64	1	1	2

Bowling

O	M	R	W
54.3	24	64	5
Avg	5WI	10WM	
10.00	-	-	

Highest score: 105 not out v I Zingari, Vice-Regal Ground, 1876
Best bowling: 3-8 v I Zingari, Vice-Regal Ground, 1875

Frank Kempster goes down in cricket history as the first man to score a century for Ireland. He reached this milestone in Ireland's twenty-ninth game, which was Kempster's third cap. Low scoring was the norm in those days and since Ireland's first game in 1855 only three men had scored 50s, including Kempster in the previous game.

Frank Kempster was the son of a soldier who spent many years in India. Frank may even have been born there – as was his sister Alice in Tamil Nadu in 1856 – but there are no records of his birth. With his family based in Galway, Frank was educated at Ennis College, Co. Clare, where there was a strong cricket XI. He entered Trinity College Dublin in November 1870.

He played on the Trinity first XI in 1872 but may have been injured as he missed the whole of 1873. The following year he topped the batting averages with 205 at 25.5, with a highest score of 85. This won him a place on the Irish XII to play I Zingari at the Vice-Regal Grounds. Going in No.7 he was run out for 0 but made 11 in the second innings as Ireland won by 15 runs.

Kempster also played against the All England XI for a Trinity past and present selection, scoring 21 and 10.

In 1875 he finished second in the Trinity averages to Trotter, scoring 350 runs at 23.5, and topped the bowling with 22 at 9.7. He again got an opportunity to play a top English side, making 10 and 13 for Trinity against the United South of England, dismissed twice by WG Grace, who also made 112. Against I Zingari he made a brilliant 65 in the second innings as Ireland won by 201 runs. He bowled first-change and took 8.2-4-8-3. He also played against IZ for the Vice Regal XI, who won by an innings mainly due to a huge sixth wicket stand between William Hone Jr (96) and Kempster (92). He was elected captain of the university in 1876, when his batting average slumped to 15.9 and his bowling soared to 40.

He had better luck with Ireland. The 1870s were a boom time for Irish club cricket but the representative side was strangely moribund. From 1869-73 they played just once, and in each of the six seasons from 1873-79 the only fixture was against IZ in the Phoenix Park. In a three-day game beginning on 22 August 1876, IZ made 278 and bowled Ireland out for 101

(Kempster 2). Following on 177 behind, Ireland had just passed this deficit when they lost their fifth wicket and Kempster strode to the crease. Using his powerful on-side game and finding support all the way down the tail, he took the game to I Zingari. He was still in the 80s when the ninth wicket fell, but Walshe of Phoenix proved an able partner and the pair put on 38 to see Kempster to his century. Although IZ chalked up the 207 required to win, the day belonged to the twenty-two-year-old Galwayman.

In his final year in Trinity he took part in the then highest partnership ever seen in Ireland. With David Trotter he put on 362 for the second wicket against Phoenix at College Park. Trotter made 234 but Kempster's share was a more modest 128. It was his only century for the club. He ended the season with 224 at 44.4 and turned out for a final time for the Ireland side, again against IZ, but made just 3 and 6.

His elder brother Joseph was capped twice for Ireland in 1869, and his son, Jack, won two caps for Ireland in 1920-22.

Eric Leslie Kidd

RHB, LB; Cambridge University, Middlesex, Phoenix and Ireland (1921-30)

100 GREATS

Leslie Kidd abandoned the prospect of captaining England when he took a job in Dublin in 1914. Once war ended, however, he was a prolific all-rounder for Phoenix and scored 5 fifties in six games for Ireland. He was quite a catch for his club, which is famed for its ability to sniff out talent in recent immigrants to the capital.

Until the outbreak of the First World War, the bespectacled Kidd was close to selection for the England Test team. The son of a man who played once for Kent, Leslie played for Cambridge for four years from 1910, the same year he made his first appearance for Middlesex. The following summer, going in at No.8 for the county, he made a chanceless 150 not out in two and a half hours against Hampshire at Lord's.

By 1912 he was clearly on the road to a Test cap, taking 60 wickets and scoring 856 runs. He was picked for the Gentlemen against the Players for the first time (37 and 4-97), as well as the Gentlemen of England v South Africa and the South of England v Australia, in which he made 63. He was captain of Cambridge that summer and filled that role at Middlesex when Warner was absent.

The following season Kidd was fourth in the first-class averages with 1,049 runs at 49.57, but there were no Test tourists that year or in 1914 and despite *The Times* saying he was ready not only to play for England but to captain his country, Kidd's chance was gone.

With a first from Cambridge in mechanical science, Kidd joined Guinness just before the outbreak of war. He joined the army and moved to Ireland after the war to work at St James's Gate. He joined the Phoenix club in time for the commencement of league cricket in 1919. Over the next eleven years – although he only played seventy-four games – he made 3,155 runs at 40.97, including six centuries. He helped the club to four league titles in the five years from 1921-25.

Kidd was quite able to make the step up from club cricket to the county championship and continued to turn out for Middlesex for a few games every summer until 1928. In the two-day matches of 1919 he made 100 v Surrey and 92 v Essex. For Middlesex he scored 1,848 runs (19.05) and took 44 wickets (23.93), and in all first-class cricket he made 5,113 runs (24.94), with six centuries and took 186 wickets (24.83), with best figures of 8-49 for Cambridge against Sussex.

Born: 18 October 1889, Westminster, London
Died: 2 July 1984, Dun Laoghaire, County Dublin

Mts	Inns	NOs	Runs
6	11	-	376
Avg	50s	100s	Cts
34.18	5	-	3

O	M	R	W
103.1	13	460	23
Avg	5WI	10WM	
20.00	1	-	

Highest innings: 73 v Scotland, College Park 1925
Best bowling: 5-63 v MCC, College Park 1924

As a batsman he had a strong defence, showing bowlers little of the stumps. He was a brisk scorer, however, and hit the ball hard. He bowled slow leg-breaks with a high action. His Ireland career was curtailed by his county commitments and he only played six times from 1921-30, all in Dublin. His 11 innings are worth printing: 66; 57, 20; 73, 68; 5, 1; 0, 14; 4, 68. He only bowled in seven innings but took 5-63 in the first innings he did so, and finished with 23 wickets. Against Scotland in 1925 his contribution of 2 fifties, 4-48 and 2-46 was the key to a 179 run victory.

He was a very correct cricketer but not averse to some gamesmanship. Once, when tossing for innings with Bob Lambert of Leinster, Kidd spun the coin and told Lambert to call. 'Harp' replied Lambert – naming the reverse of the Irish coin – and harp it was. 'We'll bat,' said Kidd. 'But I called harp', said Bob. 'Never heard of it', replied Kidd, 'It's either heads or tails. We'll bat.' And bat they did.

He moved back to London in 1937 but retired to Dun Laoghaire in 1967 where he died, just short of his ninety-fifth birthday, in 1984.

Raman Lamba

RHB; Delhi, North Down, Woodvale, Cliftonville, Ardmore, India and Ireland (1990)

Born: 2 January 1960, Meerut, Uttar Pradesh, India
Died: 22 February 1998, Dhaka, Bangladesh

Batting

Mts	Inns	NOs	Runs
4	4	-	62
Avg	50s	100s	Cts
15.50	1	-	2

Bowling

O	M	R	W
22	2	114	1
Avg	5WI	10WM	
114.0	-	-	

Highest score: 52 v New Zealand, Downpatrick 1990
Best bowling: 1-40 v New Zealand, Ormeau 1990

The inclusion of Raman Lamba in this list is somewhat controversial but then the Indian was no stranger to that during his playing career so there is no reason to think it would be any different today.

As a confident twenty-four-year-old Lamba joined the North Down club in Comber, near Belfast, in 1984 and instantly made a big impression, scoring more than 300 runs in his first four matches. As a professional player, his presence always divided people between those who wanted to defend the amateur status of the game in Ireland and those who wanted to see the best players, no matter what the cost.

However, there were few who could argue that he was not worth the financial investment. He was an entertaining batsman, full of big on-drives and flashing cover drives, wristy and always with a flourish. Clarence Hiles, writing in his book *A History of Senior Cricket in Ulster*, said: 'He was fiery and combative when bowling and a brilliant fielder in any position but when he batted he was confident, relaxed and focused.'

In his first season at North Down he scored more than 1,400 runs and took 40 wickets. He smashed 166 not out against Malahide in the Irish Senior Cup, leading the then cricket cor-

respondent for *The Irish Times* Sean Pender to question the right of overseas professionals to play in the competition. Partly as a result of the controversy, the Irish Cricket Union decided to exclude overseas players from the event the following year.

Lamba won four Test caps for his native India and played a total of 32 one-day internationals, with a top score of 102 against Australia in the 1986-87 series. It was thought that he never had the technique to make it as a Test batsman but his wonderful eye, ability to improvise and desire to dominate bowlers meant he was always entertaining.

He was described by *Wisden* as a 'flat-track bully' and 'a lion in his own den' and while he may have been short on technical ability he was very long on bravado and used to strut out to the middle with the air of a man about to take the bowling apart. And in Irish club cricket he often did just that.

In 1990 he became the first non-qualified Ireland cricketer to play in the NatWest Trophy (against Sussex at Downpatrick) and in total he played just four times for Ireland. He scored one half-century against the touring New Zealanders (again in 1990 at Downpatrick) and would like to have played more but he was not always a welcome presence.

'He never felt comfortable in the Irish set-up where he felt some players and administrators were anti-professional and resented his presence in the team. And of course, he was right!' wrote Hiles.

He switched clubs a number of times in the north and was the subject of a High Court ruling upholding a decision by the Northern Cricket Union to prevent him from playing for Division 2 club Cliftonville in 1991 having already done so the previous season. Apart from

North Down and Cliftonville, he also turned out for Woodvale and Ardmore, returning home for the winter to play for Delhi. He remained prolific in Indian first-class cricket, scoring three triple centuries, 31 centuries and 27 fifties and finishing with a Ranji Trophy career average of 53.

Sadly, he was killed in 1998 at the age of thirty-eight after being hit on the head while fielding at forward short-leg during a club match in Dhaka, Bangladesh. He will be fondly remembered in many parts of Ireland, particularly around the town of Comber where he was something of a celebrity during his time at North Down.

Robert James Hamilton Lambert
RHB, OB; Leinster and Ireland (1893-1930)

It is with good reason that Bob Lambert is known as the Grace of Ireland. His achievements at cricket are comparable to WG, with whom he shared a birthday. Lambert played cricket for Ireland in five decades, and over his career made more than 100 centuries for club and country. His talent even attracted WG Grace, who persuaded him to try his hand at county cricket with London County in 1903, making 46* and 38 against Lancashire in his only game.

Lambert was a true all-rounder, his batting average of almost 28 being well clear of his bowling average (18.65). In nineteen consecutive seasons he did the double of 1,000 runs and 100 wickets, three times recording 2,000 and 200. He won many matches for Ireland with bat and ball and captained the side to four victories, a mark only beaten in the 1970s by Alec O'Riordan.

Raised in Rathmines, he attended the Rathmines School and Wesley College before he completed his education at St John's, Preston

and Edinburgh University. As a boy, he would get up for nets at seven in the morning with the Leinster professional Peter O'Connor, bowling until he could land the ball on the spot with his eyes shut.

He first came to the attention of the national press in 1890 when, barely sixteen, he made 89 not out for the powerful Leinster club against Laytown. A portrait duly appeared in the *Irish Field*, along with details of the gold medal the club presented to him. They were also impressed by the 'rattling, manly speech' he made in reply.

His heavy run scoring earned him a first Ireland cap at age nineteen, when he scored 51 against I Zingari. He was brought on tour to England three weeks later, and was an instant success, making 28 v Combined Services, 28 v Surrey and 115 batting No.7 against WH Laverton's XI. He batted with a runner throughout that maiden century due to an injury which prevented him fielding during the match.

It was the first of his four centuries, the others coming in 1904 (100 v Cambridge University

Born: 18 July 1874, Rathmines, Dublin
Died: 24 March 1956, Rathfarnham, Dublin

Mts	Inns	NOs	Runs
51	81	11	1954
Avg	50s	100s	Cts
27.91	8	4	39

O	M	R	W
1261.3	324	3227	173
Avg	5WI	10WM	
18.65	12	4	

Highest innings: 116* v Philadelphia, College Park 1908
Best bowling: 7-11 v Scotland, College Park 1910

at Rathmines), 1908 (116★ v Philadelphia in College Park) and 1911 (103★ v Scotland in Glasgow).

Due to his studies in Britain he only became available for the full Irish season in 1898 but he had already accumulated several local records. In 1895, when he made 248★ in 125 minutes against Fitzwilliam (and took 8-23), he totalled 2,040 runs at 51 and took 209 wickets at 7. Over forty seasons he amassed 37,000 runs and took 3,700 wickets. According to teammate Pat Hone, 'his batting style was severely practical, without flourish or extraneous ornament, very quick on his feet, he was a terror to a close-in fielder; in defence he had wonderful judgement, particularly in letting the awkward ball pass him by, sometimes almost to shave the stumps, which he did with an air of apparent indifference to it.'

He studied veterinary science at Edinburgh, which resulted in him playing for Scotland against Trinity at College Park in 1898. He rose to the occasion, taking nine wickets and hitting a rapid 68, including 2 sixes into Nassau Street and two others which rattled the high railings.

He relished the challenge of good bowling and many of his best innings were against strong attacks. One of his finest innings was the 51 v South Africa in 1907 when the brilliant bowling of Vogler, Schwarz and Faulkner was repelled. He made 116★ against the 1909 Philadelphians, who included the celebrated Bart King at one end and future Australian Test 'demon' HV Hordern at the other.

Interestingly, Lambert seemed to freeze when playing at the 'home of cricket', and his five innings at Lord's yielded just 9, 11, 5, 0 and 4.

Lambert's bowling was no less brilliant than his batting: 'As a bowler, he was an extremely accurate machine', wrote Hone, 'two steps back, a sudden turn and the ball was with the batsman disconcertingly quickly, this (need I say?) without intent to bustle the striker, but as the result of his perfected rhythm.'

His off-breaks were good enough to run through sides and he took 10 or 11 in a match on four occasions. His most lethal performance was at College Park in 1910, when Scotland were set 238 to win. Lambert had come on late in the first innings and ended with 3-3, but opened second time around with GWF Kelly. Nine of the ten wickets to fall were clean bowled, as Scotland collapsed to 32 all out in 21.1 overs. Lambert finished with 10.1-4-11-7. He took seven wickets on two other occasions and other notable feats were 5-37 v South Africa (1894) and 10-72 in the match against MCC at Lord's in 1926, when he was fifty-one.

He was forty-four when the Leinster Senior League began in 1919, but his career lasted long enough for him to score eight centuries and 3,277 runs at an average of 40.45. He also picked up nine league medals, the last seven in a row up to his retirement in 1934. He won the Marchant Cup as the province's leading batsman in 1921, with the incredible average of 217. He started that season with a run of eight unbeaten innings – when he was finally dismissed he averaged 664! His century of centuries was raised against Halverstown at Rathmines in 1931, two years after he made his ninety-ninth.

He played for Ireland alongside his brother, Sep, and just missed out on playing with two of his sons. Drummond won his only cap in 1930, two weeks before Bob won his last against MCC in College Park. Ham – also a rugby international – won the first of his twenty-one caps the following summer.

Bob played for Ireland at badminton and was president of the ICU in 1931, 1932 and 1947.

WG Grace was asked if Lambert would have been an even greater cricketer had he played regularly in England. 'How do you improve on perfection?' Grace replied.

Charles Lawrence

RHB, RARM; Surrey, Middlesex, Phoenix and Ireland (1856-61)

Born: 16 December 1828, Hoxton, London
Died: 20 December 1916, Canterbury, Melbourne, Australia

Batting

Mts	Inns	NOs	Runs
12	21	1	254
Avg	50s	100s	Cts
12.70	1	-	15

Balls	Runs	Wkts
-	-	98
Avg	5WI	10WM
-	11	5

Highest innings: 50 v Gentlemen of England, Phoenix Park, 1856
Best bowling: 8-32 v MCC, Lord's, 1858

Irish cricket owes a huge debt to Charlie Lawrence, the Londoner whose entrepreneurship and vision in setting up an All Ireland XI sowed the seeds of representative cricket in the country.

Lawrence had grown up in London and Scotland – taking all ten wickets for the latter against the All England XI in 1849 – but moved to Dublin two years later to take up a professional post at Phoenix. Lawrence organised visits by the major English sides to play his club but the arrival of the Gentlemen of England in 1855 to play their Irish counterparts was the acknowledged start of Irish international cricket. The Phoenix professional was selected for the return visit in 1856, scoring a debut fifty and taking ten wickets.

He was again to the fore when the United All England XI came to Phoenix that September. The English side featured top professionals Lillywhite, Caffyn, Lockyer, Grundy and Wisden and dismissed Ireland for 116 and 71. Chasing just 62, Lawrence bowled through the innings unchanged as the Englishmen fell six runs short.

The Earl of Carlisle, Queen Victoria's representative in Ireland, enlisted Lawrence's help in building a cricket field for him on the grounds of his lodge in the Phoenix Park. They developed an excellent ground on the lawn and the Earl allowed Lawrence to organise benefit matches for his efforts as well as high profile games. The Gentlemen of England played Ireland at the Rotunda Gardens in 1857, with Lawrence again dominant (46, 14 and eight wickets) as the visitors escaped with a draw. Lawrence was always open to sport as a moneymaker, although his bid to introduce the Irish to lawn tennis proved a commercial failure.

Lawrence's finest hour for Ireland came at the home of cricket, Lord's, in May 1858. Ireland took on a good MCC side, every one of whom played some first-class cricket, and won by an innings and ten runs. The game was played in poor weather conditions – 'thick mud' according to *Lawrence's Annual* (no relation) – and Lawrence bowled unchanged as MCC collapsed to 53 all out, taking 8-32 from his 23 overs. He took 4-25 in the second innings, a match return of 12-57.

Lawrence played occasionally for Surrey and once for his native Middlesex (scoring 78 v MCC), but finally left Phoenix for Australia in 1861 as a member of H H Stephenson's touring side. He stayed on after the tour, playing for New South Wales, but returned to the UK as a manager of the Aboriginal touring team in 1868. Former Australian Test player and historian Ashley Mallett wrote that 'perhaps he more than any other person could claim the title of the Father of Australian cricket'. And the same tribute could also be paid by Irish cricket.

100
GREATS

David Alan Lewis
RHB, RAM; YMCA and Ireland (1984-97)

Born: 1 June 1964, Cork

Batting

Mts	Inns	NOs	Runs
121	145	20	3,579
Avg	50s	100s	Cts
28.63	20	4	40

Bowling

O	M	R	W
483.4	38	2,238	51
Avg	5WI	10WM	
43.88	-	-	

Highest score: 136 not out v Wales, Kimmage 1990
Best bowling: 4-21 v Scotland, Stratford 1993

If enthusiasm was used as a barometer when judging a cricketer then Alan Lewis would be one of the greatest of them all. A man for the big occasion, he always seemed to raise his game as the stakes got higher, whether playing for Ireland or his beloved YMCA. In first-class matches he holds the Irish record for the highest batting average of those who played more than four matches with 53.33 and he is the only Ireland player to win man of the match awards in both the Benson & Hedges Cup and NatWest Trophy.

In domestic cricket he often reserved his big performances for the blue-riband Leinster Senior Cup, becoming the youngest player to score a century in the final in 1984 at the age of twenty. He hit 86 in the 1987 final, winning the man of the match award again. In the 1990 cup final he hit 129 not out and took 6 for 36 (all clean bowled), an all-round feat that remains the best individual performance by any player in a final of that competition. As YMCA dominated the cup through the late 1980s and early 1990s, Lewis made 124 in the 1991 final and took 5-17 in the 1994 decider.

In 1984 he became the first Irish-born player to score 1,000 runs in a Leinster club season, averaging 77.61, and also taking 40 wickets to capture the Samuels Cup for all-rounders. That was also the season he made his debut for Ireland, kicking a 121-cap career off with a first-ball duck against the touring West Indians at Rathmines, caught by Joel 'Big Bird' Garner at square leg off the gentle bowling of Larry Gomes. It is never easy growing up as the only son of an Irish international – Alan's father, Ian, won twenty caps between 1955 and 1973 – but it soon became clear that Lewy junior had more confidence and talent than Lewy senior ever had. A little like Woodvale's Stephen Warke, Lewis emerged from his father's shadow to forge a wonderful international career in his own right.

In that memorable summer of 1984 Lewis was invited to Taunton for a trial with Somerset and although he acquitted himself well, scoring a half-century against Hampshire seconds, he knew the lifestyle of the professional cricketer was not really for him. He did not like the selfish nature of county seconds matches and at that time most counties were looking for opening bowlers as opposed to batting all-rounders like him.

His time with Ireland started slowly as it took him no fewer than 23 innings to pass 50. But two half-centuries in a match against Wales gave him the confidence he needed and he gradually became a consistent performer for his country.

The following season he scored an unbeaten 82 against Gloucestershire at Bristol and he hit his first century and what turned out to be his highest score with 136 not out against Wales at Dublin ground Kimmage in 1990. Three more centuries were to follow in Ireland colours, against Gibraltar in the 1997 ICC Trophy and

twice in first-class games against Scotland. He never got out once he had reached three figures for his country.

He captained Ireland on thirty-five occasions and was always a great competitor and student of the game. His enthusiasm and fierce desire to win was infectious on the field but it sometimes meant he lost a little clarity as leader. He was criticised on occasion for taking too many risks trying to force a win although his win percentage of 24 per cent is not bad considering he was in charge of a team that was very much in transition.

'I always liked to attack as captain and there are games that I probably could have saved but I wanted to give us a chance to win them. I always wanted to win,' he said. Lewis was critical of the political nature of some selection decisions that were made during his career. He particularly remembers an occasion as captain when his club mate Angus Dunlop was left out of the ICC Trophy team in 1994 in favour of Decker Curry who hailed from the North-West.

'Angus was clearly the form player in the warm-up games but did not play in the first game, much to the amazement of then coach Davie Houghton and myself but that was a political decision and that was it. Selection at that time was dogged with it,' he said.

His own playing career ended on a somewhat sour note at the end of the 1997 season when he was left out of the team for what would have been his final cap, against the MCC at Lord's. The day before, Lewis had scored a half-century against an Earl of Arundel XI and that evening he told then coach Mike Hendrick that he would be retiring from representative cricket after the following match. Lewis was left out of the team to play the MCC in favour of youngster Peter Davy, a move that made many people angry and certainly disappointed Lewis himself, who would have liked to have called it quits with a game at the so-called home of cricket.

'I think a lot more people made a meal of it than I did at the time and I don't really blame him for that. I had great respect for Mike

Hendrick and for what he achieved as the Ireland coach. It was just unfortunate the way things worked out,' he said.

By then, though, he had other fish to fry. Upon retirement he turned his attentions to rugby and he managed to forge a very suc-cessful career as a referee and he later officiated in the 2003 World Cup as well as Six Nations, Tri Nations and other internationals. He is still involved as a sponsor of cricket in Ireland through his firm of insurance brokers, as well as on and off the pitch for YMCA.

100 GREATS

James Macdonald
LHB, SLA; Queen's University, North Down and Ireland (1926-39)

Born: 17 September 1906, Comber, Co. Down
Died: 8 March 1969, Bangor, Co. Down

Batting

Mts	Inns	NOs	Runs	
29	48	6	1196	
HS	Avg	50s	100s	Cts
108*	28.48	7	1	14

Bowling

O	M	R	W
805.6	218	1720	82
Avg	5WI	10WM	
20.98	4	-	

Highest innings: 108* v MCC, Rathmines 1936
Best bowling: 5-24 Vs Australia, Ormeau 1938

James Macdonald was the towering figure of the inter-war period in the NCU, an all-rounder of the top rank of whom England batsman Maurice Leyland said 'there's nowt wrong with James Macdonald except he wasn't born in Yorkshire'.

Educated at Connell's Institute, a commercial school in downtown Belfast, RBAI and Queen's University, he learnt the game at his hometown club in Comber. Macdonald was a left-arm orthodox bowler with a high-arm action, relying on subtle changes in flight. He first played for the North Down first XI in 1922, aged fifteen, and within two years won the first of his nine NCU cup winners' medals, to which he added six league titles.

He was still a teenager when he first played for Ireland, making 95 against Wales at Ormeau. With a touch of symmetry, 95 was the score he made on his farewell appearance against Sir Julian Cahn's XI in 1939.

103

The leading light of the great North Down team of the 1920s and '30s, he was described by Ulster cricket historian Clarence Hiles as 'frugal but penetrating as a bowler, and the stylish supreme batsman who broke the hearts of the best bowlers around'. A sample of some of his records include the cup final best of 159★ record v Cliftonville in 1935 and a cup record 197★ against CPA in the 1930 first round. He made 1,500 runs in all that season, including four centuries and 451 in the month of July alone. As a bowler he hit the heights in 1931, taking 8 in an innings on four occasions, and 13-59 in the NCU cup final.

Some authorities consider his Ireland career to have not been as productive as it should have been. He scored only one century – albeit a match-winning one – 108★ v MCC in 1936. He was not always available to the selectors, missing eighteen of the forty-seven games Ireland played between his debut and finale.

His finest performance with the ball came against the 1938 Australians at Ormeau, when he captained the side (he won three of thirteen games as skipper). In tandem with leg-spinner Eddie Ingram he bowled Australia out for 145, returning figures of 5-24 off 16 overs. The five scalps he claimed were Barnes, White, Fingleton, O'Reilly and Ward. Australian journalist Arthur Mailey, a former Test spinner himself, described it as 'the best piece of left-arm slow bowling he had seen on the tour'. His frugality throughout his career saw him concede just 2.1 runs per over.

A teammate said that the best he saw him bowl was against MCC at Lord's in 1935, bamboozling batsmen that included Nigel Haig and Bill Edrich. The umpire was astonished at this Irishman, remarking 'If Verity could bowl as 'e's bowlin' now, Aussies wouldn't have a chance.'

He scored 7 fifties for Ireland, four of them against MCC whom he faced eleven times without being on the losing side. His best match performance came at Lord's in 1927, on his brother Tom's debut, when James took 5-57 and made 59. He had the huge honour of being selected for Sir Pelham Warner's XI to play England Past & Present in September 1939 but the outbreak of war prevented the game taking place.

He served in the war as a Lieutenant-Colonel with the Royal Artillery, narrowly escaping death at Dunkirk, and was awarded an OBE.

He was a notable hockey international, winning twenty-five caps as a 'sound, left half-back and determined tackler'. He captained Ireland twice and was a member of the 1933 triple crown winning side. He also played for the Great Britain XI.

Ill health meant he never played cricket again after the war. He became headmaster of Regent House Grammar School, Newtownards. He was an Irish selector from 1945-60 and ICU president in 1954.

Thomas John MacDonald

RHB, LB; North Down, Queen's University, Cambridge University and Ireland (1927-9)

Born: 27 December 1908, Comber, County Down
Died: 23 March 1998, Middlesbrough, England

Mts	Inns	NOs	Runs
17	27	1	738
Avg	50s	100s	Cts
28.38	3	3	8

O	M	R	W
8	2	16	0

Highest innings: 132 v Scotland, Raeburn Place 1928
Best bowling: 0-6 v MCC, Lord's 1929

Tom Macdonald's cricket career was over-shadowed by his more accomplished brother James, but he richly deserves a place in this book in his own right. When his Ireland career ended in 1939, his seventeen appearances had seen him make three centuries, just one short of the record of the great Bob Lambert.

When the 1938 Australians ran through Ireland for 84, Tom played a gritty, determined innings and was the only one able to cope with the leg-breaks of Bill O'Reilly and Frank Ward. He batted for an hour and a quarter for 28 while Eddie Ingram was the only other cricketer to make double figures.

Like James – who was two years older than Tom – he was first selected as a teenager. His debut at Lord's was inauspicious (though James made a fifty and took five wickets in an innings), but he was retained for the next game – the famous victory against the 1928 West Indians. He failed again but the selectors' perseverance was rewarded when he made a tremendous 132 against Scotland in Edinburgh, equalling the Irish fourth-wicket record partnership with George McVeagh.

The following summer he was run out for 67 at Lord's and two days later made 101 against the Civil Service Crusaders at Chiswick. On three further visits to Lord's he made 2 fifties and rounded off his Ireland career with 106 at Sir Julian Cahn's ground, Loughborough Road, Nottingham, in August 1939. The war ended his Ireland career and his average of 28.38 was excellent for the time, although he played in only seventeen of the forty-two games between debut and finale. A quirk of his career was that all three of his centuries were scored away and all three of his fifties came at Lord's. His highest score in Ireland was just 28!

He was a vital element of the all-conquering North Down side that dominated the NCU from the mid-20s to the mid-30s. He won six league medals and nine cups, and usually made an important contribution. He made the only fifty of the match at Ballynafeigh to win the 1928 cup, and made 108 against Ulster CC in the 1931 final at Ormeau. His leg-breaks were useful too, his 4-12 and 39* being decisive against Armagh in the 1932 final.

Thomas John MacDonald
continued

Many of his finest performances were in tandem with James. For Queen's University he made 189 in 1928, destroying a strong Trinity team alongside his brother, who took 13 wickets. In 1935 the pair made centuries in a partnership of 224 against Donacloney.

He went to school at RBAI and after Queen's he studied at Cambridge, playing one first-class game for the university in 1930. Opening the batting he made 29 and 7 against Somerset. Thomas Macdonald died in England in his ninetieth year.

Noel Cameron Mahony
RHB; Bohemians, Dublin University, Civil Service, Clontarf and Ireland (1947-53)

Born: 15 January 1913, Fermoy, County Cork

Mts	Inns	NOs	Runs
9	17	1	299
Avg	**50s**	**100s**	**Cts**
18.69	-	-	5

Highest score: 42 v Yorkshire, Ormeau, 1948

Noel Mahony was a leading figure in Irish cricket for most of the twentieth century, as player, captain, and administrator. But it is for his extraordinary work in pioneering cricket coaching in Ireland that he deserves to be ranked among Ireland's cricketing greats.

Born in a Cork market town before the Great War, Mahony spoke with reverence about being inspired by watching the wristy play of Duleepsinjhi, nephew of Ranji, who made an unbeaten 168* for Cambridge Crusaders against Cork County in 1926.

Mahony was educated at the King's Hospital in Dublin, where he captained the senior team for three seasons from 1930. Besides a short period when he learned his trade at Trinity, it was to be a lifelong relationship with the school, where he taught mathematics.

He joined the nearby Civil Service club and made his senior debut for that club in 1934. He was at Trinity from 1933-37, playing fourteen times for the first XI, but the bulk of his career in Dublin was spent at Clontarf, where he played from 1938 to 1955, with a handful of games in the early 1960s. He spent many school summer holidays in Cork, where he turned out for County and Bohemians.

He was a steady opening batsman, capable of the sheet anchor but, once set, a prolific scorer. He made 5,904 senior runs for Clontarf, at an average of 33.54, topping the provincial averages in 1944 (526 at 37.57) and 1952 (534 at 59.33). He scored the first of his four centuries, an unbeaten 100, in a total of 199-1 declared, at Claremont Road. YMCA scored 114-0 to force a draw!

In 1946 he made 104 to win the cup semi-final against YMCA, but his 69 in the final against Phoenix was a losing battle. He won senior cup medals in 1943 and 1950.

In 1937 he performed the probably unique feat of appearing for Leinster v Ulster in July and for Munster v Leinster in August. With six years robbed by the war, his Ireland career was late starting. He made a good debut at Lord's, his 31 and 40* helping Ireland to a seven-wicket win, while he also impressed in sharing in opening stands of 83 and 42 with clubmate Louis Jacobson. After an excellent 42 in a rain-affected draw with Yorkshire, he was elevated to the captaincy for only his third cap.

He had a short tenure, winning two and drawing two of his six games in charge. His teams beat Scotland in 1948 and 1949, but defeat in 1951 saw him lose the captaincy and

his place in the side. He came back for one more cap two years later but was never picked again.

It was the arrival of Jimmy Angell of Hampshire as coach to King's Hospital in 1933 that inspired Mahony to coach. 'From him I got my first lessons in, and first love for, pure cricket coaching, and that love has never left me.' Mahony became the first NCA qualified coach in Ireland and spread the gospel through the land with a network of apostles. He was national coach of the ICU for many years and in his retirement coached the Irish women at their first World Cup in Australia in 1985. He was also an inspirational influence on the Trinity side of the late 1980s that was the most successful for the college in the last thirty-five years.

He was a noted sportsman, playing interprovincial table tennis and captaining Greystones and Hermitage golf clubs. In his eighties he frequently shot less than his age and had a hole-in-one at the age of eighty-six. He was ICU president in 1979.

Herbert Martin

RHB; Lisburn and Ireland (1949-68)

100 GREATS

Herbie Martin was a central part of the post-war glory years of Lisburn Cricket Club in the late 1940s, '50s and '60s. At that time the club's Wallace Park ground would be filled with hundreds of spectators on a Saturday afternoon keen to watch Martin and other Lisburn heroes such as Jack Simpson, Jack Bowden, Tom McCloy and George Crothers. As these players gradually departed they were replaced with a seemingly never-ending supply of quality in the shape of men such as Cecil Walker, Jimmy Corken and later, perhaps the best of them all, Dermott Monteith.

They won the NCU Challenge Cup eight times during that period and the league many more times, including three years in a row from 1950-52. And in the middle of this was Herbie Martin, a graceful and hard-hitting middle-order batsman who had the ability to adapt his

game as the need arose during a match. He was an excellent team player who knew how to pace an innings and he was also renowned for his catching and ground fielding skills.

Martin played thirty-nine times for Ireland in a career that spanned nearly twenty years from 1949 to 1968. He made a quality 61 in just his third game, against Nottinghamshire at College Park, Dublin and looked to have settled well into life at the higher level of the game in Ireland. But a period of indifferent form that followed meant he was in and out of the side for a couple of seasons. His top score of 88 came against Scotland in Edinburgh in 1956 and although he never got to 100, he managed to pass 50 on eight occasions, ending with a career average close to 20.

He was a younger brother of Tommy Martin, who had played three times for Ireland during the 1930s. Tommy was an opening bowler who

Herbert Martin
continued

Born: 4 May 1927, Lisburn

Mts	Inns	NOs	Runs
39	74	5	1,282
Avg	50s	100s	Cts
18.58	8	-	31

Highest score: 88 v Scotland, Raeburn Place 1956

could move the ball both through the air and off the pitch and he took 6 for 97 on debut against the Sir Julian Cahn's XI at Ormeau. Sadly, he was not to fulfil his promise as his life was cut short by tuberculosis at the young age of twenty-six.

Herbie Martin played his final game for Ireland in 1968, a drawn match against Scotland in Glasgow and he stayed with Lisburn CC until 1972. He was an excellent all-round sportsman having played in goal for the Ireland Schools hockey team and he also played rugby for Instonians and Ulster, being selected for one Irish trial as a back-row forward.

A highly qualified physicist, he was awarded his Ph.D from Queen's University Belfast in 1955 and settled well into life as an academic. In 1972 he emigrated to Brisbane, Australia to take up a lecturing post and, although long retired now, he still lives Down Under.

Mohammad Afzal Masood
RHB, RM; Phoenix, Rush, Coleraine, Malahide and Ireland (1982-88)

When Alf Masood arrived on the Leinster cricket scene in 1980, he brought a rare flash of colour in every sense of the word. His batting prowess was immediately obvious and he rapidly made his way onto the North Leinster and Ireland teams.

Mohammed Afzal Masood was born in Lahore in 1952, and made his first-class debut as a schoolboy for Lahore Reds. In Pakistan he also played at the top level for Sargodha, Punjab

University, Lahore and Pakistan International Airlines. He was a brilliant batsman, making two centuries in a match for Pakistan under-19s against England under-19s (including Bob Willis) before he got a chance to try his hand at Northamptonshire in 1972. He made 929 runs and scored 6 fifties for their second XI but a contract did not materialise.

He remained in England until 1980 before moving to Dublin to set up a chain of boutiques.

Born: 2 May 1952, Lahore, Punjab, Pakistan

Mts	Inns	NOs	Runs
40	55	5	1940
Avg	50s	100s	Cts
38.80	11	4	7

O	M	R	W
86.4	13	361	6
Avg	5WI		
60.17	-		

Highest innings: 138 v MCC, Lord's, 1985
Best bowling: 3-30 v Worcestershire, Beechgrove, 1988

On joining Phoenix, Masood began shattering club and provincial records: He made an inter-provincial all-time best 196★ for North Leinster against South Leinster before the game ended when the opposing captain told a young bowler to fire down four wides. Four years later he made the second highest interprovincial score, 178 against Ulster Country. His average at this level is 69, the next best just 41.

Masood was picked for Ireland in 1982, ten years after his last chance at big-time cricket. He took his chance from the off, making 39★ and 57★ against MCC on his debut at Eglinton. He made his maiden century in only his third game, against Wales at Rathmines.

His six years in the Irish side saw him score 1,940 runs, including four centuries, becoming the first to score tons in successive matches. His average of 38.80 is the best ever for a completed career. In eleven games against Wales, Scotland and MCC he scored 904 runs at 50.22, and Ireland never lost. Masood's century at Lord's in 1985 is recalled as one of the finest ever made for Ireland – he was out ten minutes before lunch on the first morning, with 138 runs to his name.

Masood, who always batted in specta-cles, also made a memorable hundred against Gloucestershire two years later, the first by an Irish player against a county side. His other century came against the Duchess of Norfolk's XI at Arundel in 1985. He was the first Irish batsman to score 500 runs in a season, making 543 in 1986 and 546 in 1987.

One of his most satisfying innings for Ireland was the 69 he made against Sussex in 1983 at Clontarf. Masood became the first Irish player to claim a man of the match award in the NatWest Trophy and he certainly impressed Sussex's Imran Khan, then captain of Pakistan. 'You haven't lost it at all, I can see no change', he told Masood in the middle and tried to per-suade him he could have a future at Test level, but Masood was content in Dublin. In 1987 the nations met in a pair of one-day games at Rathmines, both of which were easily won by Pakistan. In the second game the hard-hitting Masood blitzed 6 sixes and 13 fours on his way to 89 off 82 balls.

Utterly dominant when set, Masood also made 204★ for Phoenix v The Hills, the first

three Leinster league medals, two league cups and a cup winners medal in 1982. He formed a lasting partnership with the veteran DR Pigot, the extension of whose senior career into his sixties was largely due to having Masood at the other end scoring freely.

He was a very useful bowler at club level, bowling medium pace in-duckers. He took half his six wickets for Ireland in one innings, returning 3-30 against Worcestershire at Beechgrove in 1988.

His career was often controversial: he was banned for two games in 1983 for defying an ICU edict that players must stand down from club matches on the eve of internationals. In 1988 his international career ended when he committed a similar offence by playing for Coleraine. He was not averse to WG Grace-style gamesmanship either. He was clean bowled by Trinity student John McGrath with the first ball of a senior league game, but complained – unsuccessfully – that he wasn't ready for the delivery.

The latter stages of his career were blighted by further controversy when an attempt to play as a professional for Rush – then a junior side – was blocked by the Leinster union. He ended his senior career, aged fifty, in Malahide. He made 9,477 runs in Leinster competition, including 23 centuries, at a then record average of 51.22.

limited overs double century in senior competition. He won man of the match in the 1986 Irish Senior Cup final when Phoenix became the first Leinster club to claim the trophy. He won

Alexander McBrine
RHB, SLA; Donemana and Ireland (1985-94)

Like many of the best Irish cricketers, 'Junior' McBrine was born into it. It was in his blood with his father Alex having been a stalwart member of the Donemana club in the North-West and his brothers and cousins also playing to a high standard. And if that wasn't enough he also attended Strabane High School in the North-West, one of the top academies for the game in the country.

But Junior was the brightest star in the expansive McBrine sky and it became clear from an

early age that he was the one to look out for. By his mid-teens he had broken into his club's first team and at the age of sixteen he took 8 for 22 against old rivals Sion Mills in a league game, bringing him to the attention of selectors for Ulster and Ireland underage teams.

In total the burly, square-jawed McBrine ended up with thirty-five caps over a ten-year period, a tally that would surely have been greater but for availability problems. Primarily a left-arm slow bowler who could bat effectively

Born: 16 September 1963, Omagh

Mts	Inns	NOs	Runs
35	37	8	654
Avg	50s	100s	Cts
22.55	1	1	13

O	M	R	W
558	117	1,783	44
Avg	5WI	10WM	
40.52	-	-	

Highest score: 102 v Scotland, Coleraine 1987
Best bowling: 4-38 v Matubeleland, Bulawayo 1986

in the lower middle order, McBrine was a tough, canny operator who used variety to great effect, mixing up his line, length, flight and pace to confuse all but the best batsmen.

It is remarkable that as a Donemana man he played around 50 per cent of his matches on one of the smallest grounds in the country and yet, even as a spinner, he has consistently been at or very near the top of the bowling averages in North-West club cricket.

But while he dominated the world of club cricket, McBrine was never able to trouble top batsman on a regular basis for Ireland. His bowling average of nearly 41 says little of the talent and application that he had as a representative player. It didn't help of course that he mostly played in an Ireland team that was going through a period of transition in the years after the legends of Dermott Monteith, Ivan Anderson and Alec O'Riordan had retired but before the first full-time professional national coach Mike Hendrick really made his mark.

His best figures came on a tour of Zimbabwe in 1986 when he took 4-38 against Matabeleland at Bulawayo, and later in the tour he dismissed Graeme Hick in a game against a Zimbabwe President's XI at Harare. Of course, it should be noted that Hick was on 309 at the time.

As it turned out, McBrine often contributed more effectively with the bat than the ball. His average of 22.55 is not bad for someone considered to be more of a bowler, although in 37 innings he only managed to pass fifty on two occasions. He made 102 batting at No.9 against Scotland at Coleraine in 1987, putting on 150 for the eighth wicket with Simon Corlett and making sure Ireland had an innings lead when, at one stage, they were struggling at 102 for 7. It remains the lowest position for any Irish century-maker.

He was also an excellent fielder, particularly in the slips, using his shovel-like hands to great effect. 'I saw Junior take five slip catches and win man of the match in an Irish Senior Cup final for Donemana one year,' says Barry Chambers of CricketEurope. 'Three of them were brilliant. If any Test player took them you would say it was amazing,' he said.

William Kyle McCallan

RHB, RAO; Cliftonville, Waringstown and Ireland (1996-)

100 GREATS

In July 2005 Kyle McCallan (whose birthday is the same as that of Don Bradman) took over as Ireland's most-capped player, breaking the record of 121 set by Alan Lewis in 1997. It is a career that spanned the first three of Ireland's full-time national coaches, Mike Hendrick, Ken Rutherford and Adrian Birrell, and he was one of the most important players to the Irish team during that time.

Having shown good promise with his club Cliftonville, McCallan began in the Irish side as an opening batsman who turned his hand to a little orthodox off-spin. Coming on as the seventh bowler used in his debut match against Wales in Rathmines in 1996, McCallan took a wicket with his first ever ball for his country. But he was really in the team as a front-line batsman and in just his second international, against the MCC at Malahide, he showed what he could do by scoring his maiden century for Ireland.

But gradually during his career, McCallan slipped further and further down the batting order and he has now batted everywhere from one to nine in the full senior side. Indeed, had he batted in the 2005 Intercontinental Cup final against Kenya at Windhoek, it would have been at ten. For his first few seasons he was an opener. Then, when he took over as captain in 2000, he mostly batted in the middle order at five or six and since then as Ireland's batting line-up grew stronger, McCallan made way to become a very effective lower-order striker. But as his batting became less central to the team's success, his bowling took centre stage.

He is a clever bowler who never lets batsmen get on top of him and has a knack of turning up at crucial moments to take wickets or strangle a run-chase. There have been plenty of career highlights. He bowled Brian Lara out for a duck in a NatWest Trophy match against Warwickshire at Edgbaston in 1998. In the 2005 ICC Intercontinental Cup final against Kenya in Namibia he captured figures of 4 for 34 on a dead-flat pitch, including the prize scalp of Steve Tikolo, to give Ireland the chance of victory which they duly took by six wickets.

And in 2006 he took wickets with his first two balls and ended with figures of 4-3-5-3 as Ireland beat Gloucestershire in the C&G Trophy, the first time they had beaten a county side in a competitive match away from home.

Always a thinking cricketer, one of McCallan's strengths is that he knows his own limitations. While batting he plays only the shots that he knows he can play well and cuts the others out and his bowling is all about building pressure on batsmen with a nagging line and length rather than trying to turn the ball square and risk giving up bad balls.

'I think I have played with cricketers who have an awful lot more talent than I have but maybe my strength has been my discipline in that I have not tried to become too flamboyant and do things that are out of my control,' said McCallan.

Surely one of the noisiest men in Irish cricket, McCallan's enthusiasm for the game and never-say-die attitude has kept his teammates' spirits up even at low points. Whether from the sideline to the batsmen or on the pitch to his fellow bowlers and fielders, his constant encouragement can be heard far beyond the confines of the ground itself.

Born: 27 August 1975, Carrickfergus

Batting

Mts	Inns	NOs	Runs
145	136	19	2,827

Avg	50s	100s	Cts
24.16	10	2	41

Bowling

O	M	R	W
1326.1	167	4,934	155

Avg	5WI	10WM
31.83	1	-

Highest score: 100 not out v MCC, Malahide 1996
Best bowling: 5-23 v Italy, Ayr 2000

After being handed the captaincy in 2000 while still only twenty-four, McCallan led Ireland thirty-five times with a win-rate of 40 per cent. But while he was a thoughtful and at times inspirational leader, unfortunately his captaincy will always be associated with the disastrous ICC Trophy of 2001 in Toronto. With Ireland hopeful of coming in the top three and thus securing a place in the 2003 World Cup in South Africa, they had a string of disappointing defeats to the USA, United Arab Emirates, Denmark, Scotland and the Netherlands and ended up coming eighth.

Coach Ken Rutherford, a former New Zealand Test captain, was heavily criticised following the ICC Trophy as were the selectors who had picked certain players who were clearly carrying injuries into the tournament and duly broke down. And although McCallan continued to lead Ireland until after the Triple Crown competition that summer, by the end of the season Jason Molins had taken over as captain.

'The period of Irish cricket in which I was captain was very unsuccessful and for that I have to take my portion of the responsibility. I saw it as a huge honour. I tried my very best but it didn't happen for various reasons, some of which were my fault and some of which were not,' he said.

It is possible that he was made captain too early in his playing career and that his tenure would have been better four or five years later when he was more experienced on the field and more confident when it came to matters of selection and other off-field involvements.

But as a popular figure within the game in Ireland, it didn't take McCallan long to re-establish himself in the side as just an ordinary member of the team and it gave him the freedom and time to focus on the job he was being asked to do as a player. He was appointed vice-captain later in Molins's tenure and retained that position when Trent Johnston took over the side at the end of the 2005 season.

Adrian George Agustus Matthew McCoubrey

RAF, RHB; Ballymena, Essex, Saffron Walden and Ireland (1999-)

Born: 3 April 1980, Ballymena, County Antrim

Mts	Inns	NOs	Runs
43	23	11	53
Avg	50s	100s	Cts
4.42	-	-	5

O	M	R	W
376.5	42	1,400	52
Avg	5WI	10WM	
26.92	-	-	

Highest score: 11 v Berkshire, Finchampstead 2002
Best bowling: 4-17 v Scotland, Mannofield 2005

A right-arm bowler of genuine pace, Adrian McCoubrey had the ability to strike terror into the hearts of all but the best batsmen. When his dander was up he could cause real problems by putting the ball just short of a length and putting doubt in batsmen's minds as to whether to go back or forward to him.

However, problems with consistency, question marks over his fitness and the quality of his fielding and the fact that he offered little or nothing with the bat meant that he was often left out of Ireland sides in favour of more all-round performers.

The Ballymena boy made his debut in the full Ireland team in 1999 as a nineteen-year-old against Scotland at Ormeau and made an instant impression taking 3-38 and 1-40 as Ireland beat their old rivals by four wickets. He became a fixture in the side after that as the fastest bowler in Ireland. His steady and smooth run-up leads into quite a complicated twirling delivery style that generates real pace but it has also put undue pressure on his back and lower limbs meaning

that he has suffered from niggling injuries from time to time.

He was a member of the Ireland squad for the disappointing 2001 ICC Trophy in Toronto where Ireland failed to qualify for the 2003 World Cup in South Africa. Like most of the team, McCoubrey was inconsistent, doing well against Bermuda, the Netherlands and Canada but was much less impressive against the United Arab Emirates (0-41 off 4.4 overs) and Scotland.

After a couple of trials with Essex in 2002, the twenty-two-year-old was signed by the county but despite playing several games for the first team at Chelmsford, he never really established a permanent place there and was released two years later.

McCoubrey returned his attentions to the Irish team and set about helping them to qualify for the 2007 World Cup in the West Indies and also the ICC Intercontinental Cup in Namibia in 2005. He took 3-19 against Uganda during the group stages of the ICC Trophy in Comber, County Down but was later dropped for the semi-final and final as Ireland just missed out on overall victory to Scotland at Castle Avenue, Dublin.

A few weeks later he put in perhaps his finest performance in Ireland colours to date against

Scotland in a three-day Intercontinental Cup match at Aberdeen. It was a low-scoring match on a green wicket at Mannofield and heading into the fourth innings it looked like the competition's defending champions Scots would close the game out, needing just 135 to win and more or less book their place in the world finals in Windhoek that October.

But in an eight-over spell of real ferocity McCoubrey removed four of the Scottish top order with just 13 runs being hit off him (plus four no-balls), including the form players Ryan Watson, Fraser Watts and Neil MacRae. He threw everything into it and although he had obviously put on weight since his stint as a full-time professional cricketer at Essex, it was probably as fast as he ever bowled. Sometimes McCoubrey could be a difficult character to work out amid bouts of apparent moodiness but then captain Jason Molins knew how to get the best out of him.

'Give me another over,' Molins told a puffing McCoubrey with the Scots three down for little more than 30. 'And this time I want you to run in properly.'

McCoubrey, visibly upset by this perceived slight on his workrate, steamed in the following over, taking the edge of Colin Smith's bat and putting the Scots in serious trouble at 34 for 4. Ireland went on to win by three runs and they made it to Namibia beating Kenya in the final.

McCoubrey still lives in England and continues to play in the Essex league.

100
GREATS

Paul McCrum

RHB, RAM; Lurgan, Waringstown, North Down, Lisburn, Muckamore, Dunmurry, Armagh, Laurelvale and Ireland (1989-98)

Born: 11 August 1962, Waringstown

Batting

Mts	Inns	NOs	Runs
74	53	30	355
Avg	50s	100s	Cts
15.43	1	-	22

Bowling

O	M	R	W
938.4	147	3,426	106
Avg	5WI	10WM	
32.32	1	-	

Highest score: 63 v Wales, Usk 1991
Best bowling: 5-52 v MCC, Malahide 1996

A consistent and deceptive right-arm bowler, Paul McCrum was one of Ireland's top performers with the ball during a period of transition in the 1990s. Having made his debut relatively late for an opening bowler, at the age of nearly twenty-seven, in all McCrum won seventy-four caps between 1989 and 1998 and is one of only fourteen players to take more than 100 wickets.

McCrum bowled with a quick action that was all arm and because his left arm did not work as hard, batsmen often assumed to their cost that he was slower than he was. But his unconventional, whippy technique generated more pace than it seemed to and the ball would invariably be on the batsman sooner than they thought.

'He never let Ireland down and on his day he was as good as anyone that I played with,' said former Ireland teammate and captain, Alan Lewis.

He took 106 wickets for Ireland during his career, including 5-52 against the MCC in 1996 in a match where he took eight wickets in all.

A bit of a nomad in terms of club cricket, McCrum played for many clubs in Ulster including Lurgan, Waringstown, North Down, Lisburn, Muckamore, Dunmurry, Armagh and Laurelvale, effectively turning out as a professional cricketer for many years.

As a lower-order batsman, McCrum was capable of making important contributions coming in at nine, ten or jack for Ireland. His top score of 63 came against Wales in 1991 when he put on the lion's share of a vital 58-run tenth-wicket partnership with Eddie Moore. As No.11 batsman in 1997, he put on an unbeaten 100 for the tenth wicket with Dubliner John Davy, finishing with 44 not out to Davy's 51 not out. It is still an Irish record for a final wicket stand.

Younger brother Charles played twenty-two times for Ireland between 1990 and 1994, taking 25 wickets at an average of just less than 30 and scoring 567 runs at 25.77, with a top score of 70 against Scotland in 1992.

Andrew McFarlane
RHB, OB; Sion Mills and Ireland (1934-39)

Andy McFarlane is a cricketing legend in the North West, and the fact that he only won five caps is still a sore point around Sion Mills way. For decades the clubs around Belfast and Dublin had dominated the Irish selection process and the far-flung provinces didn't get a look in. Eventually the prolific McFarlane forced his way into the reckoning and became the first born-and-bred North Westerner to play for Ulster and, in 1934, Ireland. At 35, it was too late for Andy and he never showed what he was capable of.

Donald Shearer, the Englishman who also had to overcome anti-North West bias, described him thus: 'Andy's bat always looked broad – just as Hammond's did and Cowdrey's too; he saw the ball so soon in its flight that, although he was not noticeably quick on his feet, he was always in position to play the correct stroke – and he had plenty of those. His sense of timing was exact and the ball travelled very fast off his bat'.

He attended Sion Mills Public Elementary School and picked up the game through spending all his spare time on the cricket field. War meant he was almost 20 when he got his chance in senior cricket and made an instant mark. He took 8-13 against City of Derry, including a hat trick, in the first match of the 1919 season and when he made 75 against the same opponents to win the league play-off, he was chaired off the field.

A strong team was assembled including Hughie Donaghey and John Flood, but it was McFarlane who was to the fore over the next quarter century as Sion dominated cricket in the union, claiming eight senior cups and 13 leagues. He scored his first senior hundred (128* v St Johnston) in 1921 and topped the averages in most seasons. In all he made 22 senior centuries, the biggest of which were 227 v Strabane in 1933 and 180 v Brigade in 1931. He made three of them in 1937 when he averaged 115.25.

Born: 21 June 1899, Sion Mills
Died: 14 June 1972, Londonderry

Batting

Mts	Inns	NOs	Runs
5	8	1	73
Avg	50s	100s	Cts
10.43	-		2

Bowling

O	M	R	W
14	2	38	1
Avg	5WI	10WM	
38.00	-	-	

Highest score: 27 v Sir Julian Cahn's XI, Loughborough Road 1937
Best bowling: 1-38 v MCC, Sion Mills 1934

His first cap was against MCC on his home ground in 1934, the first time an Irish side played in the North-West and the first time a native North-Westerner played – after almost eighty years of representative cricket. He made 0* and 1 in that game and took a wicket, but was overlooked again for three years. In the summer of 1937 he won four caps – a couple of 20s being his best performance – and after another in 1939 that was that.

Sion Mills entered the NCU Challenge Cup in 1947 and won it on the first attempt, the only time a North-west side has won it. They brought a great deal of support to Ormeau for the final against Armagh, who ran up 238 in the first innings. McFarlane made a fine 117 alongside Flood (87) to give Sion a lead of 81.

The forty-eight-year-old veteran turned to his off-breaks and claimed three wickets to set his side 126 to win, which they achieved in a tumultuous finish. He retired three years later.

Knowledgeable observers were convinced he could have excelled in bigger fields. 'Andy was the batsman who most impressed me', wrote Scott Huey, 'had he been given a chance to play in county cricket I feel he would have proved himself a truly good player'. Shearer believed, 'He would have made a name for himself in first-class cricket as all the potential was his.'

While his batting feats were most notable, he was a fine bowler too. Most seasons he took 50 wickets with slow, flighted off-spin. In 1927 he took 77 wickets and he took nine Waterside wickets for 19 two years later.

Trevor George Brooke McVeagh

LHB; Dublin University, Phoenix, Ireland (1926-38)

Born: 14 September 1906, Drewstown, Athboy, County Meath
Died: 5 June 1968, Dublin

Batting

Mts	Inns	NOs	Runs	Avg
21	36	5	1108	35.74
HS	50s	100s	Cts	
109	7	-	17	

Highest innings: 109 v Scotland, Greenock 1932

George McVeagh was not only one of Ireland's greatest cricketers but probably the country's greatest all-round sportsmen. He represented his country in four sports – and in cricket, hockey and tennis he is rated in the highest rank.

Despite only taking up the game at university, he was an ever-present on the Irish hockey team from 1933-39, winning a triple crown in his first season and three more as captain from 1937-39. He won the Irish squash championship from 1935-37 and won his only cap in 1937. From 1933-38 he was the star of the Davis Cup team – it reached the semi-final in 1936 – and he returned in 1948 to win a doubles at age forty-two. He played twenty-one matches in all, winning seven. His finest feat in tennis was twice beating the great Wimbledon champion

Bill Tilden. It was his skill at tennis that took him away from cricket when he finally had to choose between the summer games.

His finest hour in cricket came as a student on his home ground of College Park. Educated at St Columba's, he was first capped as a teenager and had four caps under his belt when he was picked on the side to play the West Indies. Batting at No.8 he came in with Ireland on 92-6 in the second innings, a lead of just 123. The fair-haired left hander gave no openings as he combined for partnerships of 81 and 106 with fellow students Heaslip (44) and Thornton (37) to see Ireland to 320. In three and a half hours at the wicket he hit 10 fours in making 102 not out. He then held four catches – two exceptional – as Ireland dismissed the tourists for 291.

McVeagh was a prolific batsman at club level and scored a record 3,282 runs for Trinity, including nine centuries. Four of those – three in succession – came in 1927 when he won the Marchant Cup for the leading average in Leinster.

McVeagh's skill with rackets seems to have proved useful in cricket as he mastered the smash-through cover at full stretch! Not a textbook batsman, he drew criticism for his tendency to leave a gap between bat and pad, and keeping his head over the ball was never a priority. DR Pigot Sr described his methods as 'unorthodox, indeed almost uncouth'. It was a very effective style, however, and his masterful eye brought him

1,108 runs at an average of almost 36, which puts him in the top five of Irish players.

He was consistent, too, and rarely failed. It was his twelfth innings for Ireland before he made a score less than 14, and he followed his 102★ v West Indies with 65 and 56★ against Scotland. He made an unbeaten fifty at Lord's in 1929 and followed with 94 against the Civil Service Crusaders. In 1932 he made his second century against Scotland in a remarkably similar manner to the first and with the same result. His record in second innings – 578 runs at 48.2 – was far greater than his first, which is the reverse of what usually occurs. He took just 31 innings to reach 1,000 runs for Ireland – the fastest until Alf Masood in 1986.

In his mid-twenties McVeagh began concentrating on tennis and won just nine cricket caps from 1930 to his retirement in 1938. He returned to cricket in 1958 when he was elected president of the ICU and his nephew, Donald Pratt, also played for Trinity, Phoenix and Ireland, as well as being a squash international. Later a successful if controversial solicitor, he died suddenly aged sixty-two after playing tennis with Davis Cup player Cyril Kemp.

100 GREATS

John Michael Meldon
RHB, RM; Dublin University, Phoenix, County Galway and Ireland (1888-1910)

Jack Meldon was a giant of nineteenth-century Irish cricket, although his statistics might not suggest as much. His Irish career spanned twenty-two years and included two tours of North America, the second of which he organised himself.

His father, brother, uncle and five first cousins played first-class or international cricket and he was educated at Beaumont College, St Stanislaus Tullabeg and Clongowes. A combined Tullabeg/Clongowes side toured Dublin in 1885 when young Jack impressed with 75 against Phoenix. He entered Trinity to study law in January 1887 and although his record there was mediocre to begin with, he was brought along – aged nineteen – to the US and Canada where he made his Ireland debut.

He scored a fine 69 against All New York and did well against Philadelphia when they visited Dublin the following summer. It wasn't until his fifth season in the college XI that he made a century, but as that was an unbeaten 208 against Phoenix he can be forgiven. The early '90s saw Meldon at his peak, making several big centuries against the Curragh Brigade, and he was captain of Trinity for an unparalleled three seasons from 1890-92. He made his highest score for Ireland – 92 against Scotland at Raeburn Place – in 1890.

He hit another 92 against a strong Cambridge side for Trinity two years later but his form seemed to have deserted him and he rarely made a big score thereafter. Some authorities believe that, for all the correctness of his technique, he was over fond of big hitting and squandered his wicket too often taking that route.

The perennial squabble about who should select Irish sides flared again and Jack took it upon himself to raise and organise the tour to North America in September 1892. He made a fine 81 against Philadelphia, but averaged just 16 on the tour.

He played twenty games in a row for Ireland, a record until Jimmy Boucher finished his career with a run of 32. He toured England with Trinity and Ireland in 1893, with a best score of 71 against WH Laverton's XI. He was invited to play for the Gentlemen against the Players in 1895 but had to turn down the opportunity.

On graduation he returned to practice in Galway and cricket took a back seat. He rarely made the trip up to Dublin but one visit in 1899 saw him make 119 at College Park. It was a surprise when he was selected for a trial match ahead of Sir Tim O'Brien's tour of England in 1902. Harrington and Ross routed

John Michael Meldon
continued

Born: 29 September 1869, Dublin
Died: 12 December 1954, Tunbridge Wells, Kent

Batting

Mts	Inns	NO	Runs
32	49	4	897
Avg	50s	100s	Cts
19.93	6	-	8

Bowling

O	M	R	W
130	39	315	13
Avg	5WI	10WM	
24.33	-	-	

Highest score: 92 v Scotland, Raeburn Place, Edinburgh 1890
Best bowling: 4-15 v I Zingari, Phoenix Park 1891

the 'Possibles', but Jack held firm for 81 and won a recall. His tour was according to *Cricket* magazine, 'an absolute failure', and he made no more than 14 in any of his six innings.

He was recalled six years later against Philadelphia and again as captain in 1910, but failed on both occasions. One late starring role awaited Meldon – he was almost forty when he became the first Irishman to score a century in each innings, a feat he managed for Phoenix against the Royal Artillery at the Phoenix Park.

He retired to England in the 1930s and made annual visits to Ireland to fish. He died in 1954 but his death went unremarked upon in the Irish sporting press.

Jason Adam Max Molins
RHB; Carlisle, Railway Union, Oxford University, Banstead, Phoenix, Brondesbury and Ireland (1995-2005)

100 GREATS

Nobody who saw Jason Molins play from the time he was a schoolboy in Dublin's Wesley College and The High School would be surprised that he would go on to win more than seventy caps for Ireland. Nor that he would win most of them as captain.

Indeed it was his captaincy that perhaps earned him the most respect from both those involved in the game in Ireland and also his opponents. An astute tactician, his field placings were particularly imaginative and he had a knack of making bowling changes at just the right time in the context of a match.

Molins captained Ireland on a record forty-one occasions and his win rate of 63 per cent is comfortably the highest of any long-term Irish captain

Born: 4 December 1974, Dublin

Batting

Mts	Inns	NOs	Runs
76	79	4	2,138
Avg	50s	100s	Cts
28.51	13	2	29

Highest score: 107 not out v Zimbabwe, Stormont 2003

in history. He was the first Irish captain to ensure qualification for the World Cup finals when he led Ireland to the final of the 2005 ICC Trophy.

As an opening batsmen, Molins led from the front. On his day he was a devastating stroke player, who could take apart some of the best bowling attacks in the world. Chasing 292 against the West Indies in Stormont in 2004, Molins and Jeremy Bray put on 111 for the first wicket with Molins's 66 coming from just 58 deliveries.

Molins always latched on to anything over-pitched, usually driving it to the boundary but his strongest shot was probably the hook and it would have to be a high-class bouncer before he would resist swinging the bat.

One of seven members of the Irish Jewish community to play cricket for Ireland (including his brother Greg), Molins played his early club cricket with Carlisle, part of the Maccabi sports club in the south Dublin area of Kimmage. He dominated the underage ranks in Leinster cricket with the bat and at that stage was still able to cause plenty of problems with his right-arm medium pace.

As a confident teenager, he established himself on the Carlisle first team and it did not take long before he was dominating bowlers at that level just like he did in youth cricket. When Carlisle closed in 1998 Molins played for a while in Railway Union but he took up a place in Oxford University and earned his blue in the annual colours match against Cambridge, scoring 268 runs in seven first-class games.

He went to London after leaving Oxford and became an investment banker in the city.

He played club cricket locally and managed to combine captaining his country with living and working in England. He spent the 2004 season commuting back to Dublin every Friday to play for the Phoenix club, opening the batting with fellow Ireland player Bray.

In total he scored more than 2,000 runs at an average of 28.51, including a high score of 107 not out in a ten-wicket win over Zimbabwe in 2003. A fine slip fielder, he took 29 catches and never backed away from a verbal battle if he felt an opposition batsman needed some advice. In 2005 he had a disappointing season with the bat, passing 50 just once in 12 innings and there were concerns over his fitness and fielding. He missed the ICC Trophy final due to a shoulder injury and he was dropped from the squad ahead of the Intercontinental Cup finals in Namibia, with Trent Johnston taking over the captaincy. A loss of form and fitness cost him his place in the Irish side in 2006 and he was omitted from the squad for the 2007 World Cup.

Born: 2 June 1943, Lisburn

Batting

Mts	Inns	NOs	Runs
76	99	16	1,712
Avg	**50s**	**100s**	**Cts**
20.63	9	-	33

Bowling

O	M	R	W
2404.1	889	5,664	326
Avg	**5WI**	**10WM**	
17.37	27	7	

Highest score: 95 v Scotland, Titwood 1984
Best bowling: 8-44 v MCC, Lord's 1973

Dermott Monteith was a gifted, attacking left-arm slow bowler who remains without doubt one of the best players Ireland has produced. In seventy-six matches he took a record 326 wickets at an average 17.37, including no fewer than 27 five-wicket hauls and 7 ten-wicket matches. In 1971 in a remarkable three-match run he took 6-33, 7-45, 6-84, 7-42, 5-26 and 6-40. This was followed by another eight wickets in a match against the MCC at Lord's.

While he was blessed with great skill and an astute cricketing brain, Monteith was not the easiest of players to get along with and was not always the most tolerant of his teammates' failings.

'Dermott was a brilliant player and he couldn't always understand why the rest of us didn't do the things on the field that he was able to do,' said former Ireland teammate Roy Torrens.

Monty, as he was known, was never short on confidence. In 1977 he genuinely rated himself as the third best left-arm spinner in the world after Indian legends Bishen Bedi and Dilip Doshi. Then he saw Doshi play in Ireland that summer and, not being overly impressed, moved himself up to number two on the pecking order. In truth, he probably privately believed he was better than Bedi too.

His best bowling figures for Ireland came against the MCC at Lord's in 1973 when, having taken five in the first innings, he caused even more problems in the second, bowling 31 overs and taking 8-44 as Ireland ended up winning the match outright by seven wickets. Indeed, his match figures of 13-93 remain the fifth best by an Irishman and the Lisburn man also holds the number three spot with 13-78 against the Combined Services in Portsmouth in 1971, the number six spot with 13-126 against the Netherlands in Castle Avenue, Dublin, also in 1971, and the number eight spot with 12-56 against Wales at Rathmines in 1973. For one man to hold four of the top-ten best bowling figures, in matches spanning the 150 years of the Ireland national team, is remarkable indeed.

He still holds first and second place for the number of wickets taken in a season. In 1971 he took 47 wickets in just five matches at an average of 8.36 and in 1973 he took a further 46 in four matches at 5.67. Considering they play in the region of twenty matches per year these days (albeit mostly one-day games) it is impressive that he still holds that record. In terms of bowling average, of those who played thirty times or more for Ireland, Monteith's 17.37 is second only to the great Jimmy Boucher's 15.26.

He had a short but successful period with Middlesex where he filled in for spinners John Emburey and Philippe Edmonds who were regulars on the England team at the time. Indeed, it was said that he could have had a successful professional career in England for most other counties, which were not so lucky as to have two international-class slow bowlers as Emburey and Edmonds.

He captained Ireland on thirty-seven occasions (with a win ratio of just over 30 per cent) and demanded nothing but 100 per cent commitment from his players on the field of play. He captained like he bowled – always attacking and never afraid to take a chance. Perhaps unlike some of his teammates, Monteith never felt inferior to the opposition no matter who they were and he always backed his own ability and that of his teammates. For example, he chose to bat first at Lord's against Middlesex in Ireland's first ever match in what was then called the Gillette Cup in 1980, despite the fact that they had the likes of Wayne Daniel, Emburey, Wilf Slack, Vintcent van der Bijl and Mike Gatting in their side.

'There was no thought of damage limitation when he was confronted with teams full of Test players,' said former Ireland teammate Mike Halliday. 'His team talks were direct and to the point and he would not speak for half an hour if one minute would do. On one occasion, before taking the field at Rathmines against the West Indies, his urgings to his side amounted to an instruction to 'consider yourselves whipped up'.

Monteith was a larger-than-life character and enjoyed a packed social life, especially on cricket tours and even in the middle of games. On one occasion during a match against Worcestershire at New Road, Monteith was rooming with fellow slow bowler Mike Halliday.

'Rooming is not quite the correct word as

Dermott seldom used bedrooms,' said Halliday. 'At the close of play we were both batting and both on nought not out. The following morning, myself and the bleary-eyed Monty set out to face Norman Gifford at 10am and I did not give us much chance of saving the match. Half an hour later, I was still nought not out but Monty was smacking the ball all around the ground.' The match was saved.

Indeed, although he will be remembered as a slow bowler who used flight and guile to great effect, his batting was more than useful in the middle to late order for Ireland. He scored nine half-centuries, including one on debut in 1965 against the MCC at Lord's, and he made his highest score of 95 against Scotland in what turned out to be his last international match in 1984. Having hit 1,712 runs at an average of nearly 21, he is rated as Ireland's best all-rounder ahead of Alec O'Riordan and Garfield Harrison.

He is the only player to score 100 runs and take ten wickets in the same match (26 and 78, 7-38 and 5-57 against Scotland at the Mardyke in 1973).

In 1985 an accident involving a hit-and-run driver ended his career and although he was over forty by that stage, it is generally believed that he could have continued playing at that level for some time. He still remained involved in Irish cricket, first as a selector for the national side and later as president of the Irish Cricket Union in 1999. He wrote a memoir entitled *A Stone from the Glasshouse*, a unique insight into the cricketing life of one of the most colourful and talented Irish players of all time.

Paul John Kevin Mooney

RHB, RAM; North County, The Hills and Ireland (1998-)

100 GREATS

Born: 15 October 1976, Dublin

Batting

Mts	Inns	NOs	Runs
82	68	24	765
Avg	50s	100s	Cts
17.39	1	-	19

Bowling

O	M	R	W
639	68	2,729	106
Avg	5WI	10WM	
25.75	-	-	

Highest score: 66 not out v Club Cricket Conference, Shenley 2003
Best bowling: 4-12 v Scotland, Ormeau 1999

On his day, and with the right conditions, Paul Mooney is capable of causing real problems with his nagging brand of medium-pace seamers. The rest of the time you can rely on him to do a steady job, putting the ball on a good line and length time and time again. To score off him, batsmen need to take chances and on pitches where he can get a bit of lateral movement, he picks up wickets.

One of Ireland's most consistent performers from the time he made his debut in 1998, Mooney remains one of the fittest players in the side. Brought into the side by then national coach Mike Hendrick, Mooney established himself quickly and the following year took 4-12 off 11 overs against Scotland in a first-class match at Ormeau as the Irish won outright by four wickets.

Along with his extended family, Mooney was a member of the Balrothery club in north Dublin that later merged with Man o'War to form North County. At that time in the mid-1990s North County was one of the weaker senior clubs in the Dublin area and at the age of fifteen Mooney was already expected to do a job for the first eleven against the best players in Leinster cricket.

Frustrated with what he saw as the disorganisation of cricket at North County and their consequential poor results, the ambitious Mooney left and joined nearby The Hills, which was doing much better in the domestic leagues. He subsequently returned to County and has enjoyed plenty of success with the now formidable Balrothery club. Overlooked by national selectors at all levels of underage cricket, Mooney was perhaps a victim of the tail-end of discrimination against those unfashionable clubs in north Dublin who produced some fine players who never got the representative honours they deserved.

Hendrick's arrival as national coach changed all that. Not interested in reputations or fashions, the no-nonsense former England Test bowler demanded the best possible group of players available regardless of where they came from. He spotted Mooney, liked what he saw and drafted him into the squad towards the end of the 1997 season, although he only won his first cap against the MCC at Lurgan the following June.

Although he has not yet taken five wickets in an innings, he has five four-wicket hauls, including 4-24 against Zimbabwe at Castle Avenue, Dublin, in 2000.

Playing against Namibia in 2006 he took his one-hundredth wicket for Ireland, a feat only thirteen other bowlers in the history of Irish cricket have achieved. Like most pace bowlers of a certain age, in recent years he has struggled with back injuries and other muscle problems but he is still one of the sharpest fielders in the Irish squad and a very safe pair of hands, particularly in the deep.

Although primarily regarded as a bowler, Mooney is a much under-rated batsman. In fact, his first two caps were as a middle-order batsman who occasionally bowled and while now he usually bats at No.9 or No.10 for Ireland, he still has the mentality of an all-rounder. When the wicket falls to bring him to the crease, he always runs out to the middle with the look of a focussed and serious batter and the fact that he has only scored one half-century for his country is more down to his batting position than his abilities, bat in hand. He has been left stranded not out one-third of the times he has batted. Batting at No.10 in the 2005 ICC Trophy final at Castle Avenue, Mooney put on an unbeaten 55 for the tenth wicket with Gordon Cooke as Ireland fell 47 runs short of Scotland.

A hard-working player who is passionate about Irish cricket, Mooney is seen as a genuine team player, prepared to make personal sacrifices for the greater good. 'He's the sort of guy you want to go to war with,' said national coach Adrian Birrell.

100 GREATS
Eoin Joseph Gerard Morgan
LHB, RAM; North County, Middlesex and Ireland (2003-)

The youngest player to make this list, Eoin Morgan looks to have a very bright future in the game although it also looks like that future will not be in his native country. Having been spotted by Middlesex, Morgan now spends most of his summers plying his trade in London although he has still been free to play for Ireland through most of the 2005 and 2006 seasons.

A member of a cricket-mad family from north Dublin, Morgan's brothers and sisters also play the game and after stints with Rush and Malahide, the youngster settled on North County, consistently one of the strongest clubs in Ireland over recent years.

He became the youngest player to be capped for Ireland on 20 August 2003 when he was

Eoin Joseph Gerard Morgan
continued

Born: 10 September 1986, Dublin

Batting

Mts	Inns	NOs	Runs
28	26	1	876
Avg	50s	100s	Cts
35.04	6	1	16

Highest score: 151 v United Arab Emirates, Windhoek 2005

still twenty-one days short of his seventeenth birthday. His record has since been beaten by Lisburn leg-spinner Greg Thompson but unlike Thompson, Morgan has cemented his place in the side. He was run out for nought in his debut match against Free Foresters at Eton College but the following day he made a classy 71 and has been a regular fixture since then, clearly a favourite of coach Adrian Birrell.

'As far as I have seen, Eoin Morgan, along-side Ed Joyce, is the best batsman that Ireland has produced,' said Birrell. 'He has a wonderful technique and has dominated Irish cricket at every age group and is now starting to dominate at senior level also. He has made a lot of hundreds for someone his age.

'He is very confident and very easy to coach. He is a very good team man. He is a good fielder and a good scholar of the game for a young guy. I would think he has a very, very bright future in the game, full-time.'

That full-time future has already begun at Lord's where he is highly rated by such Middlesex legends as Mike Gatting and John Emburey. He already has a first-class century to his name, having made 151 for Ireland against the United Arab Emirates in the ICC Intercontinental Cup semi-final in Windhoek, Namibia in 2005. He also made 93 while batting alongside his county-mate Joyce to secure victory over Bermuda in the ICC Trophy at Stormont earlier in the same year.

He captained Ireland at the 2006 ICC Under-19 Cricket World Cup in Sri Lanka, ending up as second highest run scorer in the competition with 338 at an average of nearly 68. His chanceless 124 against New Zealand in the draining Colombo heat and humidity was perhaps the finest innings of the tournament.

A technically very sound left-handed batsman, Morgan has a high back-lift and when in form, he has a straight drive to rival any player in the world. Although his batting is the reason for his selection, he can also bowl medium pace away swingers and is an athletic fielder, particularly at slip or in the covers. His serious attitude towards training is consistent with his desire to forge a long career in the professional ranks of the game in England.

Henry George Hill Mulholland
RHB, RM; NICC, Cambridge University and Ireland (1911)

Born: 20 December 1888, Ballyscullion Park, Bellaghy, County Londonderry.
Died: 5 March 1971, Bellaghy, Co. Londonderry

Batting

Mts	Inns	NOs	Runs
1	1	-	149
Avg	50s	100s	Cts
149.0	-	1	-

Bowling

O	M	R	W
13	3	44	0
Avg	5WI	10WM	
-	-	-	

Highest score: 149 v Scotland, Glasgow, 1911

Hon. Sir Harry Mulholland played just once for Ireland and like Robert Gregory, his one day in the sun was a warm one. Mulholland scored 149 in his only innings, against Scotland in 1911, and never played again. At the time it was the third highest innings ever made for Ireland, although it is now ninth in that list since a flurry of big scores in the twenty-first century.

Mulholland was a Cambridge blue, playing in three Varsity matches. He made just one fifty, his 78 in 1912 being the key to victory, while he also captained the university to another win in 1913. He played thirty-one games for Cambridge, scoring 1493 runs including three centuries, the best of which, 153, came against the 1911 Indians. He also took 51 wickets, including 5-9 v Middlesex at Fenner's.

Harry and his brother Edward (who also played for Cambridge) used to run a cricket week on their own ground at Ballywalter Park, Co. Down, recruiting many English players to take on Na Shuler and the Free Foresters.

'A powerful and effortless hitter, whose straight drives arriving at the bowler, head high and with extreme venom, curving in the air like a low, sliced, golf drive, remain in my memory', wrote Pat Hone.

His only Irish cap – as a late replacement – was at the Hamilton Crescent ground in Glasgow, when he opened the batting. After losing his partner George Morrow, he added 130 for the second wicket with Dickie Lloyd and 132 for the third with Bob Lambert. He hit 5 sixes and 15 fours and the total of 409 for 4 declared was only the second time that four hundred had been passed.

Mulholland was later appointed Speaker of the Northern Ireland House of Commons from 1929-46 and became the first Baronet of Ballyscullion. Mulholland's feat was also attained by three other men on debut and all four share the distinction of never again reaching three figures. They are an often tragic quartet and none were to stay long in the green-trimmed sweater.

Croose Parry was an Englishman who had played twice for Warwickshire in 1908 and 1910 before settling in Cork. He was first capped, aged thirty-nine, against Scotland in 1925, and marked the occasion with 124 and 39. He played twice more that season, and again in 1930, six months before he died at the age of forty-five.

Sam Edgar's short life included two games for Ireland in 1934. The Lisburn batsman was just twenty when he made 103 and 0 against MCC at Sion Mills and 32 and 0 against the same side at Trinity a week later. He wasn't selected again and died, aged twenty-three, in 1937.

Jimmy Gill was a surprise selection to play for Ireland against MCC in 1948. Never a prominent batsman in a star-studded side, he had started the season with Leinster's second XI but was enjoying a purple patch of 4 fifties in six games when the time came to select a side for the Rathmines fixture, the final game of the season. The selectors went for the thirty-six-year-old home-club batsman who was in form, and they were duly rewarded. He edged the second ball from Hopper Reid to leg slip where Enthoven dropped him, and on he went to 106, following it with a 0. By the time the next Irish side was to be selected Gill was struggling and never got another chance.

Alan Norris Nelson ——————————— 100

RHB, RAM; Waringstown and Ireland (1988-94)

Born: 22 November 1965, Banbridge

Batting

Mts	Inns	NOs	Runs
44	29	15	150
Avg	50s	100s	Cts
10.71	-	-	13

Bowling

O	M	R	W
719.5	145	2,113	74
Avg	5WI	10WM	
28.17	1	-	

Highest score: 23 not out v Scotland, Myreside 1990
Best bowling: 5-27 v Scotland, Castle Avenue 1989

Had Alan Nelson of the Waringstown club in County Armagh been a little quicker, he would perhaps have been one of the best Irish bowlers of all time. His stubborn accuracy and unfailing ability to put the ball on a consistent line and length meant that he was rarely, if ever, taken apart, even when playing against the very best. But a tendency to collapse on his action meant he did not bowl from his full height and probably lost pace as a consequence.

He was not an out-and-out wicket-taker but could always be relied upon to open the bowling and get the side off to a solid start. He was particularly effective in the one-day form of the game and would pick up wickets when batsmen got frustrated with his nagging length and took undue risks.

He made his debut for Ireland in 1988, taking four wickets in a match against the MCC at Downpatrick, and was a regular choice until he retired at the early age of twenty-eight in 1994 due to injury. In that time he clocked up forty-four caps, taking 74 wickets at an average of 28 with an economy rate of less than three runs per over. His best bowling figures were 5-27 off 21 overs (including seven maidens) against Scotland in a first-class match at Castle Avenue in 1989. But he was more known for tying the top-order down rather than running through them, often ensuring that his less consistent teammates bowling at the other end picked up the wickets as batsmen decided to take them on instead.

He could have played longer but a series of injuries influenced his decision to hang up his boots while he was still capable of doing a job for Ireland.

'He was undoubtedly the steadiest medium-pace bowler of the past fifteen-twenty years,' said former Ireland teammate and fellow opening bowler John Elder. 'He was a metronome of a bowler who was economical even against the best. But I always felt he lacked a bit of self-belief,' said Elder.

'I don't think I ever remember Alan Nelson bowling a bad spell for Ireland during my time,' said another former teammate Alan Lewis. 'Along with Simon Corlett, he would have been the stand-out bowler for me in terms of accuracy in the seam department. Nelson's only Achilles heel was that he didn't have out-and-out pace but he was one of the fiercest competitors I ever played with. If I was picking an international side of players from my era, he would be first on the team-sheet,' said Lewis.

In a NatWest Trophy match against Derbyshire in 1989, Nelson registered figures of 2-19 off 12 overs, most of those runs being nicks to third man, as the Waringstown man hit the seam on a green-top at Derby. Despite getting the home side out for just 145 – having had them 85 for 7 at one stage – Ireland collapsed in reply and fell 63 runs short.

'He was a great character and I had a massive amount of time for him as a person and as a player. There were some Irish players who were unpredictable, you didn't always know what to expect from them from one game to the next. With Alan Nelson, you always knew what he would give you and he was great to have in the team for that reason. He got every ounce out of his ability and I love cricketers like that. He will never have an epitaph: 'Could have done better.' He was a quality bowler,' said Lewis.

Brendan Anthony O'Brien
RHB; Railway Union and Ireland (1966-81)

A stylish batsman and wonderful all-round sportsman, Brendan O'Brien – known universally as Ginger – played fifty-two times for Ireland in a career that promised so much more than it eventually delivered.

In domestic club cricket, O'Brien's record speaks for itself. He played for the Railway Union club in Dublin during six decades from 1959 until his final senior game in 2001. In that time he clocked up 705 matches and scored 21,765 runs,

making him the highest run scorer in the history of Leinster cricket by about 7,000 runs.

A free-scoring, right-handed batsman, O'Brien looked to dominate bowlers and was one of the most feared club players of his generation. When he was on form, which was very often, he demonstrated this by his straight drives and his fours all along the ground through midwicket.

'Ginger was a brilliant batsman with strokes everywhere around the ground,' said his former

Born: 2 September 1942, Dublin

Bowling

Mts	Inns	NOs	Runs
21.25	9	-	41
Avg	50s	100s	Cts
52	86	9	1,636

Highest score: 72 v Wales, Swansea 1977

Railway Union teammate and former Irish Cricket Union honorary secretary Derek Scott.

He was an all-round sportsman, playing professional soccer for Shelbourne FC in Dublin, mostly in the wing-half position. When he retired from football he took up hockey at Railway Union and quickly became a more-than-useful inside forward for his club. He was even selected to play for Leinster at interprovincial level.

O'Brien had a good cricketing brain although he never really enjoyed captaining Ireland, which he did on four occasions, registering two defeats and two draws. He retired just before the 1981 tour to Britain when Michael Halliday took over at the helm.

For a top-order batsman of fifty-two caps, O'Brien should probably have a better playing record for Ireland and the fact that he never scored a century for his country undoubtedly counts against him. In all, he scored 1,636 runs at an average above 21 and his top score of 72 came against Wales in 1977, one of nine times he passed 50 for Ireland.

'Personally I was disappointed with Ginger's international career,' said Scott. 'I think he was capable of doing it at that level but for some reason just didn't do it. It was a great shame because he was a fine, fine player.'

Even after retirement from the playing side of the game he has contributed greatly to Irish cricket simply by being the father of some very talented children. His sons Niall and Kevin (who have inherited Ginger's trademark red hair as well as his cricketing talents) are current Ireland internationals with Niall spending several years as a full-time county professional with Kent. Some of O'Brien's other sons continue to play cricket for Railway Union while his daughter Ciara is an Ireland hockey international with the same club.

He is a regular spectator at the Railway Union club in the Sandymount area of south Dublin and also at Ireland games where he keeps a close and loyal eye on the fortunes of his sons.

Niall John O'Brien

WK, LHB; Railway Union, Kent and Ireland (2002-)

Born: 8 November 1981, Dublin

Batting

Mts	Inns	NOs	Runs	
26	26	8	892	
Avg	50s	100s	Cts	Sts
49.56	3	3	45	5

Highest score: 176 v United Arab Emirates, Windhoek 2005

In some ways, Niall O'Brien is the typical wicketkeeper. A cheeky presence behind the stumps, not afraid to tell a batsman where he is going wrong during an innings, O'Brien is certainly someone you want with you rather than against you. His over-exuberance has landed him in trouble with disciplinary committees – he was banned for one match by the ICC after insulting the groundsman during a 2006 Intercontinental Cup match against Scotland at Aberdeen, for example. No one could ever accuse him of lacking in self-confidence – an unsuccessful attempt to reverse sweep Shane Warne on nought while playing for Kent in 2005 was captured by TV cameras and while it was certainly an injudicious shot to be playing of perhaps the finest spin bowler the world has ever known, it did demonstrate O'Brien's unfailing belief in his own ability.

And in truth, he is not short on talent. The son of fifty-two-times capped Brendan 'Ginger' O'Brien, Niall was born into a sports-mad family whose summers were dominated by cricket and winters by hockey, both at the Railway Union club's Park Avenue grounds in south Dublin.

O'Brien's sister, Ciara, is a regular in the Ireland women's hockey team while his younger brother, Kevin, made his cricketing debut for Ireland in 2006. Indeed, Kevin became just the fifteenth man in history from any country to take a wicket with his debut ball in one-day internationals as Ireland took on England at Stormont in July of that year.

After representing Ireland at the 2000 U/19 World Cup in Sri Lanka, Niall continued to improve and made his full international debut at the 2002 European Championships, which Ireland were hosting.

It was a slow start to his Ireland career, scoring 65 in his first five innings, but he was keeping wicket in his usual tidy manner and never looked out of place at that level. The following match was against the MCC at the Mardyke in Cork and O'Brien scored a fine 111, cementing his place in the side. It soon became clear that Ireland's biggest trouble was not going to be how best to bring O'Brien on as a player but rather how to hang on to him. He played the 2003 season with Ireland but was already being looked at by teams further afield and he was eventually brought into the Kent set-up as cover for their PNG-born, Australia-raised but England-qualified Geraint Jones.

Since then, O'Brien's contributions to the Ireland cause have been sporadic but also hugely important. He made a vital 58 not out as Ireland chased 292 to beat the West Indies at Stormont, Belfast in 2004 and centuries in the semi-final and final of the Intercontinental Cup against the United Arab Emirates and Kenya in Namibia in 2005 went a long way to securing victory for Ireland. His 176 against UAE in that semi-final remains the third-highest-ever individual score for Ireland (behind Jeremy Bray's 190 in the same match and Ivan Anderson's 198 not out against Canada at Toronto in 1973). O'Brien can also boast one of the highest all-time individual batting averages with 49.56, having scored 892 runs in 26 innings.

As Jones became more important to England, O'Brien was needed more and more by Kent and as such, his availability for Ireland has been limited. Under pressure from his county bosses, he opted out of Ireland's ICC Trophy campaign but it is thought that he will be available for the 2007 World Cup in the West Indies. When Jones was dropped from the England team in favour of Chris Read for the third Test against Pakistan at Headingley in August 2006, it freed O'Brien to play for Ireland during their victorious European Championship campaign. In their seven-wicket win over Italy in Glasgow, O'Brien took six catches, equalling the record for an Irishman in a single innings, set by Paul Jackson against Scotland in 1984.

Sir Timothy O'Brien
RHB, LM; Middlesex, England, Cork County and Ireland (1902-07)

Tim O'Brien is unique in being the only man to captain both Ireland and England, but he was a singular figure in many other ways too. He was one of the key players in a golden age of batsmanship and would have appeared in many more than six Tests had there not been just Australia to play for much of his career. WG Grace was once asked who was the first batsman he would pick on his dream team, replying famously 'Give me Arthur' (Shrewsbury). Less well known is that Grace went on to say, 'then give me Timothy'. A dynamic batsman who was particularly strong in forcing shots through the off side, O'Brien is remembered as one of the most colourful exponents of the batting arts in an era replete with talent.

Born into a family of publicans and politicians – his grandfather was given a baronetcy for being Lord Mayor when Queen Victoria visited in 1849 – he learnt his cricket at public school in England. He was called up by Middlesex as a schoolboy wicketkeeper but did not impress. In 1883 he went up to Oxford to try to make the grade and scored 92 on debut, against the

Australians no less, as the students recorded a famous victory. Within eight weeks O'Brien was in the Test side, dismissed twice by the 'Demon' Spofforth for 0 and 20.

He didn't play in the Test on the 1887-8 tour of Australia, but played at Lord's the following summer when he made 0 and 4 as England were all out for 60 chasing 121. He went to South Africa in 1895-96 and captained the side in Hawke's absence for the first Test. O'Brien's Test record was so poor that 20 on debut was his best score and he made just 59 runs in eight innings.

In his long first-class career (1881-1914) he made 15 centuries, the most famous of which was scored in eighty minutes against the powerful Yorkshire side in 1889. He also made 202 against Sussex in 1895, sharing a county record partnership of 338 with Slade Lucas which still stands.

O'Brien's red hair seems to have been accompanied by a fiery temperament. He was once barred from the pavilion at the Oval (which he flouted by being signed in as a guest of his butler), and also had an on-field row with Dr EM

Born: 5 November 1861, Baggot Street, Dublin
Died: 9 December 1948, Ramsey, Isle of Man

Batting

Mts	Inns	NOs	Runs
7	12	1	386
Avg	50s	100s	Cts
35.09	2	1	5

Highest innings: 167 v Oxford University, The Parks, 1902

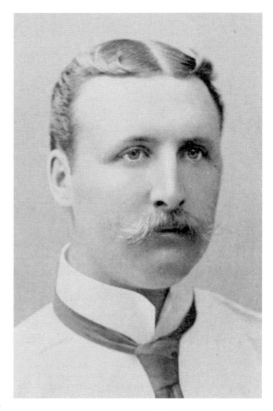

Grace. O'Brien was fed up with some negative bowling and proceeded to play aggressive reverse sweeps which almost hit EM, whose little brother WG led his county off the park. O'Brien scattered the stumps with his bat and chased the Gloucestermen to the pavilion where he offered to fight WG. The following season he presented EM Grace with a silver snuffbox in the shape of a coffin and engraved *Rem acu tetigisti* (you have hit the nail on the head)!

Most of O'Brien's relatives had remained in Ireland, where they owned land in Dublin and Borris-in-Ossory, and Timothy returned frequently. He played for Na Shuler in the 1890s and bought a castle near Fermoy. He assumed the title Sir Timothy O'Brien, third baronet, on the death of his uncle Patrick in 1892. On his retirement from county cricket in 1898 he joined Cork County. A regular visitor to the Vice-Regal Lodge, he was asked by the Lord Lieutenant to help organise an Ireland team for a short tour in 1902. O'Brien captained the team in the games against Oxford, Cambridge, MCC and London County, scoring 167 (an Irish record until 1973) against his old university. It was an important tour – the first time Ireland were awarded first-class status – and they

showed their mettle with two wins, a draw at Lord's and losing to Oxford.

O'Brien won three more caps, hitting 60* against Yorkshire in his last appearance in 1907. Extraordinarily, he returned in 1914 for one last first-class match against Oxford for Lionel Robinson's XI and rounded off his career with 90 and 111. His brother, John, played once for Ireland in 1910.

O'Brien's last years were troubled: he became embroiled in a damaging slander case which took much of his fortune. His eldest son, also Timothy, was killed in Flanders and his beloved Lohort Castle was burnt to the ground during the War of Independence. He lived for a while in Rochfort Manor in Dublin and died, at the age of eighty-seven, the oldest-living Test cricketer in the Isle of Man.

Born: 26 July 1940, Dublin

Batting

Mts	Inns	NOs	Runs
72	121	17	2,018
Avg	50s	100s	Cts
19.40	6	3	57

Bowling

O	M	R	W
1,950	639	4,503	206
Avg	5WI	10WM	
21.86	7	1	

Highest score: 119 v Denmark, Castle Avenue 1973
Best bowling: 8-60 v Netherlands, The Hague 1970

There can be little doubt that Alec O'Riordan, one of Ireland's great all-rounders, could have made a professional career from playing cricket. As a young man several county teams in England sought his signature and there are those who maintain that he could have played Test cricket had circumstances been different.

'Since 1939 when I first started watching, Alec remains the best Irish cricketer I saw,' said former honorary secretary of the Irish Cricket Union, Derek Scott. 'He might not be the best bowler, might not be the best batsman, but he was the best cricketer and the only one to score 2,000 runs and take 200 wickets.'

Born in Dublin, O'Riordan was educated by the Jesuits at Belvedere College, a nursery of

cricket with a proud tradition of shaping players for the national side. Eddie Ingram, Jimmy Boucher, John Prior, Peter O'Reilly, Owen Butler and others have pulled on the Irish sweater having passed through the classrooms of Belvedere in Dublin's north inner city.

O'Riordan made his debut for Ireland as an eighteen-year-old in a game against Worcestershire at College Park in Dublin. Not fazed by the jump from schoolboys to big boys, he scored 24 out of Ireland's low total of 102 and took a creditable 1-38 off 16 overs as Worcestershire inflicted an innings defeat. He hit an unbeaten 58 in his second match (again out of an Ireland total of 102), a drawn game against the MCC at College Park, and took 1-17 off 12 in the first innings.

As an opening bowler there were few who could match his deadly combination of pace and consistent accuracy. In seventy-two matches, he took 206 wickets at an average of 21.86 and is one of just four players to have taken more than 200 scalps for Ireland, the others being Dermott Monteith (326), Boucher (307) and Simon Corlett (233). On seven occasions he took five wickets in an innings, including a best of 8-60 against the Netherlands in 1970. His only ten-wicket match came also in that game in The Hague when he registered match figures of 12-71 off 47.1 overs. An unbeaten half-century in the first innings of that game and the fact he turned thirty on the final day made it a memorable week for O'Riordan.

A career economy rate of just 2.31 runs per over indicates how difficult he was to get away and how respected he was by his opponents. As one would expect, he dominated club cricket for Old Belvedere. He helped the club to senior status in 1956, an astonishing achievement for a club that was only founded six years previously. At 6ft 3ins and around fifteen stone, he was perhaps the most feared player in Leinster throughout the 1960s and '70s and in many ways he carried the club's fortunes on his broad shoulders for twenty years. O'Riordan's club bowling average was an outstanding 8.88, having taken 849 wickets in 372 matches. He topped the Leinster bowling averages ten times (including eight years out of nine from 1959 to 1967), he won the batting award on three occasions and was leading all-rounder seven times between 1964 and 1975.

'I worked hard,' he recalled in an interview with Anthony Morrissey for the 1986 Irish Cricket annual. 'I usually took one end for the innings… Every summer I used to wear out a heavy pair of boots and lose a stone in weight.'

But it would be a mistake to think of O'Riordan as merely a bowler who batted. He scored three centuries for Ireland and his average of almost 20 is more than respectable considering the quality of opposition they played against. Only seven batsmen have scored more centuries and he would surely have been selected even if he didn't bowl. As with many players his batting improved greatly as he got older. His first 100 in Ireland colours came against the MCC at Lord's in 1969 at the age of twenty-nine and his highest score of 119 not out was against Denmark at Castle Avenue, Dublin four years later. His last big score was as a thirty-six-year-old when he made 117 against Scotland at Glasgow. To complete the tag of genuine all-rounder, O'Riordan still holds the record of most catches by a fielder with 57. Although injuries kept him out of the side for the late part of the 1960s he recovered

to dominate the '70s and he is one of the few players never to be dropped by Ireland. He captained his country on twenty-eight occasions, winning eight and losing eight.

At times O'Riordan could come across as a player intolerant of his teammates' shortcomings and was undoubtedly an intimidating dressing-room presence for any young player. But many of those who played with him take a slightly different view.

'Playing with him at a club level we were all, to some degree, in fear and dread of his expectation of us as fielders,' said former Old Belvedere teammate and ex-president of the Leinster Cricket Union, David Williams. 'But in actual fact he was really a gentle giant and he was colossal fun to play with. Most people don't realise that he was not this big, gruff, austere, intolerant individual as he is sometimes portrayed.'

At the time when O'Riordan was contemplating offers to play professionally for English counties, there was somewhat of a dearth of quality fast bowlers in England. He would have reached his peak in the late 1960s, at the end of the Fred Trueman and Brian Statham era and before John Snow when several very ordinary opening bowlers were getting capped. Some feel that O'Riordan would have been in line for Test cricket had he chosen to move across the Irish Sea. Indeed, with the likes of O'Riordan, Dougie Goodwin and Monteith around, the Ireland team probably had a bowling attack to rival that of their more illustrious neighbour. With very few alternatives, England selectors were forced to pick journeymen county players such as left-armer Fred Rumsey and Gloucestershire's David Brown.

Alan Davidson, the left-arm bowling all-rounder – very similar to O'Riordan himself, in many ways – who played forty-four Tests for Australia and was Wisden Cricketer of the Year in 1962, said that if O'Riordan had been born an Aussie, he would have played Test cricket.

'Four counties wanted Alec and I have no doubt that if he had decided to go rather than staying in Ireland and qualifying as an engineer, he could have played for England. Alec O'Riordan was about four times as good as Fred Rumsey,' said Scott.

'For his bowling he was feared throughout Leinster and beyond,' said Williams. 'In 1979 Surrey came over to play a match and their captain Roger Knight was asked what he knew about Ireland. He said: 'I know nothing about Ireland and I know nothing about Irish cricket except one thing – O'Riordan.''

By that stage O'Riordan had retired, much to the relief of his opponents. He became a selector and, later, president of the Irish Cricket Union. It is telling that in the three decades since he played his last game for Ireland, we are still waiting for someone to replace him.

Mark William Patterson

RHB, RAM; Cliftonville, Surrey, Bedfordshire and Ireland (1995-2001)

A talented right-arm bowler of genuine pace, Mark Patterson burst onto the international scene in 1995 as a twenty-one-year-old with real promise. In his first six matches for Ireland he took 14 wickets, a feat made even more impressive considering four of those games were against top county opposition.

Patterson quickly caught the eye of scouts from across the Irish Sea and spent a couple of years on the books at Surrey. However, he never really established himself at that level, despite 6-80 on debut against South Africa A, and he was plagued by injury and a tendency to bowl wides, never really living up to the early promise he had shown and the talent that he clearly had in spades.

In forty-two matches for Ireland, he took 56 wickets at an average of less than 28 and although he never took five wickets in an innings, he managed four on two occasions, including his best bowling figures of 4-22 against Gibraltar in the 1997 ICC Trophy.

Having not played for Ireland since the end of the ICC Trophy in Malaysia, Patterson made a lacklustre return in 2001 putting in wicketless displays against the Earl of Arundel's XI and two one-day matches against the MCC at Shenley. Controversially, despite concerns about his fitness, he was selected to go with the Ireland squad to the ICC Trophy in Toronto later that summer.

It was a gamble that did not pay off. He took just three wickets during the tournament and never looked within shouting distance of his best, a contention supported by the fact that he sent down 36 wides in the 29 overs he bowled in Toronto.

A talented all-round sportsman, Patterson played soccer for the Irish Universities team while attending the University of Ulster, Jordanstown and is now a school teacher in Ipswich, England. At his best, he was an athletic and enthusiastic member of any team and was

Born: 2 February 1974, Belfast

Batting

Mts	Inns	NOs	Runs
42	21	8	157
Avg	50s	100s	Cts
12.08	-	-	10

Bowling

O	M	R	W
353.5	38	1,561	56
Avg	5WI	10WM	
27.88	-	-	

Highest score: 27 not out v USA, Kuala Lumpur 1997

Best bowling: 4-22 v Gibraltar, Kuala Lumpur 1997

capable of generating enough pace to trouble even the better batsmen on the English county scene, including Test players Michael Bevan and Craig White, whose wickets he claimed in just his sixth game for Ireland.

But while Patterson was capable of destroying teams on his day with a mixture of raw pace, excellent lines and vicious late in-swing, he was criticised for not having a plan B when batsmen got on top of him. It was said that his head would drop and he would not be able to adjust his bowling to adapt to changing situations.

He was a very useful middle-order batsman at club level although he never really got the opportunity to demonstrate that ability in the international arena. Arguably his finest hour for Ireland, however, came with bat in hand. Chasing 213 to win against the USA at Tenaga, Kuala Lumpur, the Irish were struggling at 159 for 7 when Patterson came to the wicket batting at No.9. Shortly after that Ireland needed 64 runs to win off just six overs with three

wickets remaining and with the help of Garfield Harrison and, at the very end, Greg Molins, Patterson saw the side home with five balls and two wickets to spare. His 27 not out came off just 16 balls and included 2 fours and 2 sixes. The fact that it remains his highest score for Ireland, though, would indicate how he underachieved in that area of the game, finishing as he did with an average of just over 12.

Patterson's brother Andy played sixty times for Ireland between 1996 and 2002, mostly as a wicketkeeper, and had a reputation as something of a pinch-hitter at the start of the innings. He made his top score in just his second cap, 73 against the MCC at Malahide, Dublin, batting at number three. In all, Andy scored 983 runs for Ireland at an average of 17.87. And in forty-three appearances with the gloves on he took fifty-three dismissals (43 catches and 10 stumpings), putting him fourth in the all-time wicketkeeping list. He spent a number of seasons as a member of staff at Sussex.

Archibald F Penny

Dublin University, Leinster and Ireland (1888-93)

Born: unknown
Died: unknown

Batting

Mts	Inns	NOs	HS		
13	18	7	59*		
Runs	Avg	50s	100s	Cts	
162	14.72	1	-	5	

Bowling

O	M	R	W
384	135	764	62
Avg	5WI	10WM	
12.32	4	-	

Highest innings: 59* v Philadelphia, Manheim, 1892

Best bowling: 6-22 v Scotland, Rathmines, 1888 (on debut)

Archie Penny was a teasing slow bowler who took 62 wickets in just 13 games for Ireland. His debut was the inaugural fixture against Scotland, at his club ground of Rathmines, and he took 6-22 and 2-10 as visitors routed for 65 and 51. Despite making 34 and taking 3-99 in the next game against I Zingari, he was overlooked for four years.

Although his date of birth is unknown, he was capped in 1888, three years before he entered university. He went up to Trinity in November 1891 and − 'renowned for his slow long-hops' − took 63 wickets in his debut season, at an average of 10.7. That performance won him a recall by Ireland against I Zingari, to which he responded with a match-winning 4-15 and 4-24.

Penny went on the 1892 tour to North America, where he played eight matches. A dogged tailender, his batting was at its peak on the 1892 tour, when he made his best score of 59★ against Philadelphia at Manheim. *The American Cricketer* described it as 'a fine effort', helping Ireland to 175 on first innings and a lead that saw them win by 127 runs. He made 106 runs on the tour at an average of 36 and also took 18 wickets (at 15.11).

Penny's last hurrah for Ireland came on the three-match 1893 tour of England, when he took 17 wickets, including 5-72 against the United Services at Portsmouth and 6-38 against Surrey Club & Ground at the Oval.

Penny was a key member of arguably the strongest Irish club side ever. The 1893 students won seven and drew one of their eight games against local sides; but their real stellar performances came on their tour of England when they beat Leicestershire by 135 runs, Warwickshire by 200 runs and drew with Essex. In July Oxford University visited College Park with a team that included Test players Lionel Palairet and Shrimp Leveson-Gower. Trinity triumphed by eight wickets with Penny's 8-80 the crucial contribution. He had another big day for Trinity against Gloucestershire in 1894, taking 7-105 and 3-43, including the wicket of WG Grace on both occasions. He played on the Trinity XI for three years (taking 131 wickets) but left without getting a degree.

Very tall for his era − about 6ft 2ins − he was fair haired with a luxuriant moustache. His elder brother James, to whom he bore a strong resemblance, also played for Leinster and − four times − for Ireland.

Born: 5 June 1920, Ballynafeigh, Belfast

Batting

Mts	Inns	NOs	Runs
41	73	3	1506
Avg	50s	100s	Cts
21.51	9	1	23

Bowling

O	M	R	W	Avg
1	0	2	0	n/a

Highest score: 129 v Scotland, College Park, 1951
Best bowling: 0-2 v Scotland, Paisley, 1954

S tuart Pollock was a towering figure in Irish cricket for half a century as a player, captain and ICU president. First capped as a teenager, he was unfortunate not to be able to add to his collection for seven years due to his active service in the Second World War. Fresh out of Campbell College, he was picked in the twelve to face Australia at Ormeau in 1938 but omitted on the day. The absence of six first-choice players let him in for his first cap against Scotland in June 1939, when he made 38 and 25, and he played three more times on the English tour before war broke out.

He went straight into the Ireland team in 1946, and marked it with 27 and a match-winning, unbeaten 64 against Scotland. For the next decade he was one of Ireland's leading batsmen, making 9 fifties and an excellent 129 against Scotland at College Park in 1951. Pat Hone described him as 'a very right-handed player', a powerful hooker but prone to throwing away his wicket. He was dismissed for 0 on 11 occasions.

He was one of those batsmen who are driven on by the opposition and he saved some of his best innings for games against professional sides. In 1949 Yorkshire visited Ormeau: 'Pollock's innings of 89 which took him only 75 minutes was a most brilliant one; he reached his 50 with six consecutive boundaries'. He also made an excellent 50 v South Africa in 1951 to give Ireland a first-innings lead, but his 50 v India in 1952 was not enough to avoid an innings defeat.

He was a brilliant fielder, especially at cover, and a great strength of his batting was his footwork, which was notable at Lord's in 1953 when he made 80. He bowed out in 1957 after making 64 against the Free Foresters.

Pollock came from a cricketing family and a remarkable feature of his career was how closely he followed his father Willie: both played for and captained Ireland (and both did so at Ormeau), both scored a century for Ireland against Scotland and both became ICU president. Stuart was a natural sportsman, winning international honours at squash as well as playing in Irish trials at hockey and rugby.

He won his first senior-cup medal in 1938, and added to it in 1951, 1956 and 1960, when he captained the club to the double in its centenary year, scoring a vital 72 out of 150 against Lurgan in the final. He topped the club batting averages on eight occasions, making a brilliant

John Stuart Pollock
continued

111* v Sion Mills in the cup in 1959. He was invited to play several times for MCC in big games, and made 46 v Cambridge and 82 v Oxford in first-class fixtures.

Besides 1960, he was not a particularly successful captain, winning no trophies with NICC from 1948-50 and winning just one of the ten games in which he led Ireland from 1951-55. A very active sports administrator, he was ICU president in 1980, captain of Royal County Down GC and president of the Northern Ireland sports forum.

William Pollock

RHB, RF; NICC, Holywood and Ireland (1909-25)

Born: 28 August 1886, Holywood, County Down
Died: 24 November 1972, Belfast

Batting

Mts	Inns	NOs	Runs
8	13	-	405
Avg	50s	100s	Cts
31.15	1	1	4

Bowling

O	M	R	W
131	29	306	15
Avg	5WI	10WM	
20.40	-	-	

Highest score: 144 v Scotland, Glasgow 1922
Best bowling: 4-38 v Wales, Cardiff 1923

Willie Pollock was the finest batsman of his era, but his best years were lost to the Great War and he was not always available for Ireland. In all he played just eight games over sixteen years, although they came in two spurts, 1909-10 and 1922-25. He was described in an article by long-term NCU secretary JC Picken as 'the best batsman ever produced in Ulster cricket'.

Learning the game at Campbell College, Willie Pollock started his career with Holywood CC, but increasingly played for North from 1909. He made his senior debut in 1903 at the age of seventeen and won his first cup NCU cup medal in 1905. In 1908 he made his first senior century and the following summer averaged 78 as Holywood won the league and Pollock was called up for Ireland.

He made his debut aged twenty-two against Scotland in Perth, when he made 4 and a top-scoring 47, although Ireland went down by an innings. Later in 1909 he was unable, due to injury, to travel with the tour to North America, a cause of regret to Pat Hone, who wrote that 'now that Frank Browning was getting past his best, Pollock had come to be regarded as our most finished and reliable batsman.'

He made much of his reputation in Dublin with his performances on NICC tours. In 1910 he made 173★ against Leinster and 136 v Phoenix. In 1911 he and Oscar Andrews put on 161 in forty-five minutes against the leading Dublin club, Phoenix, with Pollock making 105. He followed up with 163 against Leinster. After the Great War he played his club cricket exclusively for the Ormeau club, which he captained from 1920-25.

He played for Ireland in 1910 but not again until 1922, missing nine games. He was already thirty-five years old when he opened the batting against Scotland at Hamilton Crescent. With Louis Bookman he added 111 for the first wicket, but with only Bob Lambert (30) making a significant contribution, Ireland finished 22 behind on first innings. Pollock's 144 was more than half the team's total. He took 3-47 and scored 21 in the second innings as Ireland ran out of time, three short of victory.

The following season he made 81 against Scotland at Rathmines and was appointed captain ahead of Lambert for the visit of Wales to Ormeau in 1924. Captaining Ireland on his club ground was a great honour for Pollock (as it later was for his son Stuart), but a nine-wicket defeat ended his career in charge and he was dropped to boot.

He was recalled for the visit of MCC to Ormeau, but the game at Lord's in 1925 was his last for Ireland, his 40 helping his side to an innings victory.

He was a useful fast bowler, taking 4-38 and 2-58 against Wales in Cardiff in 1923. He also opened the bowling for Woodbrook against the 1912 South Africans in a first-class fixture. He returned 6-2-15-2, claiming the wickets of Herbie Taylor and Louis Stricker. For Holywood he took 9-14 against Waringstown in 1912.

He was president of the ICU in 1956.

100 GREATS ——————————————————— **John Andrew Prior**

RHB, RAM; Old Belvedere and Ireland (1981-86)

An enigmatic force in Irish cricket, John Prior was a batsman capable of savage destruction or limp irresponsibility. But as is so often the case for exciting players like Prior the gap between success and failure is very narrow.

A well-known schoolboy cricketer with Belvedere College, he hit a memorable 89 in the 1977 Leinster Schools Cup final and continued to impress when he joined Old Belvedere after leaving school.

He made his debut for Ireland as a twenty-one-year-old Dublin University law student but earned the last of his thirty-seven caps just five years later and apart from one wonderful season in 1984 he didn't quite fulfil his potential on the international stage.

However, he earned his place in the annals of Irish cricket and will forever be remembered for an innings of brilliance on 25 August 1982. Batting at five against a strong Warwickshire team in a two-day game at Rathmines, Prior came in with the score on 42 for 3. He passed 100 just 51 balls and 51 minutes later having despatched these first-class county bowlers to every part of the Rathmines ground and beyond. One over from England Test bowler Gladstone Small included five boundaries.

Writing in the 2006 Irish Cricket Union annual Prior recalled the day: 'The statistics will show it took 51 balls but what I can't explain is how it happened because ultimately, I think it flattered me. There was very little thought in the whole process. It was just one of those things that comes naturally. The runs came in

John Andrew Prior
continued

Born: 14 June 1960, Dublin

Batting

Mts	Inns	NOs	Runs
37	48	4	1,134
Avg	50s	100s	Cts
25.77	7	1	24

Bowling

O	M	R	W
169.5	42	568	11
Avg	5WI	10WM	
51.64	-	-	

Highest score: 119 v Warwickshire, Rathmines 1982

Best bowling: 2-7 v Scotland, Titwood 1984

big lumps – an over of bouncers on a placid pitch ended up in the gardens over square leg.

'My feet moved without being asked, it was all instinctive… I remember showering afterwards and corny as it sounds, thanking my creator for the adventure. I made a conscious effort to appreciate what had happened. I think I realised even back then that it was an episode in the nature of a shooting star – glowing brightly but only for a short time. The stars of the better players burned for much longer.' He was just twenty-four at the time and it was to be the only century he would score for Ireland.

Needless to say on the back of that performance he became a mainstay in the Irish middle-order the following year and although he didn't have a great time of it in 1983, the selectors stuck with him and he repaid their faith the following season.

In 1984, he averaged 72.75 with he and Stephen Warke scoring close to half of all Ireland's runs. ICU Honorary Secretary Derek Scott, in his annual report of 1984, wrote: 'If I dwell on John Prior's performance it is because his batting is so spectacular, different and exciting. He scored 291 runs in five innings (in 1984), 164 of his runs coming in boundaries. In all he batted for only 405 minutes.' Prior was, as ICU chairman Murray Power once recalled 'a Cavalier among Roundheads'.

In 2005 Peter Gillespie scored a century against the MCC in 47 balls, 4 fewer than Prior's legendary innings twenty-three years before. But undoubtedly Prior was facing tougher bowling and those who witnessed both say his was the more impressive.

'John was the best guy I ever played cricket with,' said former Ireland teammate John Elder. 'Wonderful talent, wonderful shot player, wonderful temperament but he always got out just when I was really enjoying watching him. So frustrating. There aren't enough John Priors in life. He could argue on any subject with you.'

Prior now lives in Australia, where he works as a business consultant for IBM. Keeping up his Jesuit connections Down Under, he coaches cricket at Xavier College in Melbourne.

Born: Bangor, County Down, 19 February 1966

Batting

Mts	Inns	NOs	Runs
52	71	3	2044
Avg	50s	100s	Cts
30.06	11	2	8

O	M	R	W	Avg
0.4	-	8	1	8.00

Highest innings: 115 v Scotland, Eglinton, 1993
Best bowling: 1-8 v MCC, Downpatrick 1992

Michael Rea won fifty-two caps for Ireland but emigrated at his peak and was discarded by an inflexible regime while at the zenith of his powers. A watchful batsman, he would dominate attacks which had been ground into submission and played many important innings for Ireland. His position at the top of the order was regularly challenged and there were only two summers when he was secure in his place.

A pupil at Bangor Grammar, he was a prolific run maker from an early age, making ten centuries for his school, and a record 977 runs in the 1983 season. Rea had played senior for Bangor from the age of fifteen and for Irish Schools for three seasons but his breakthrough innings was the 100 scored for Ireland under-23s against Leicestershire at Grace Road in August 1984. He moved to Dublin the following month and had an enormously successful career at Trinity. He made four centuries and more than 1,500 runs in four years, the second highest total ever.

His first cap came aged nineteen, as a late replacement against Scotland, when he made 5 and a composed 39. He was recalled two years later against Sussex, scoring 44 and 60 not out, but he

was in and out of the team for the next five years before a run of good scores in three-day games cemented his place. From his debut to his finale he played in just 52 of the 114 games Ireland had from his debut to finale. He was bowled only five times in 71 innings – a very low ratio – but run out 10 times, a remarkably high proportion.

After graduating he stayed in Dublin and was an important signing for Clontarf. With Deryck Vincent at the top of the order, they made several large stands for the first wicket and Rea's Leinster league and cup average of 44.26 is the highest by anyone born in Ireland. He scored a fifty every 2.67 innings, the best by any batsman until Jeremy Bray.

His first century for Ireland came against Wales in the first international at College Park for thirty years. With Stephen Warke he set a new record opening stand of 224, of which the Bangor man contributed 106. The following June Rea scored 115 against Scotland at Eglinton. He was an automatic selection for Ireland's debut in the ICC Trophy in Nairobi in

Michael Peter Rea
continued

1993, but struggled in the heat and humidity and scored a disappointing 93 runs in six innings.

Rea moved to London in 1994, but the arrival of Mike Hendrick that winter was to signal the end of Rea's career. The former England seamer demanded 100 per cent commitment from players for his 'Team Ireland' concept – travelling to all squad sessions and interprovincials – which Rea was unable to fulfil.

He was dropped on the morning of the B&H Cup game against Surrey at the Oval, which would have been his fiftieth cap. The slight fuelled the fury that drove him to score 73 against Sussex two days later, for which he won the Gold Award. He was run out for 48 against Yorkshire at Headingley a few weeks later – passing 2,000 runs for Ireland and equalling Jack Short's record of 70 innings to reach it – but only won one more cap, a duck at Southampton in April 1996. He made 4 fifties in his last six innings for Ireland.

A teammate saluted Rea thus: 'Michael Rea was great, very tenacious. Reaso was quite selfish in the way he played cricket, but that was the way to do it.'

Michael Stevens Reith
LHB, RAM; Waringstown, North Down and Ireland (1969-80)

Born: 2 May 1948, Lurgan

Batting

Mts	Inns	NOs	Runs
44	81	2	1,838
Avg	50s	100s	Cts
23.27	11	1	41

Bowling

O	M	R	W
62	21	165	1
Avg	5WI	10WM	
165.0	-	-	

Highest score: 129 v Netherlands, The Hague 1970
Best bowling: 1-24 v Scotland, Rathmines 1979

It became clear from an early age that Michael Reith, a prolific schoolboy cricketer, would end up playing for Ireland before he was too much older. An attacking left-hand top-order batsman, right-arm, medium-pace, economical swing bowler and wonderful fielder, Reith could do damage with either bat or ball at club level although he was always selected in the Irish side primarily as a batsman.

Born and raised in Co. Armagh, Reith was a product of the renowned Waringstown club and was an integral part of their success through

144

the late 1960s and 1970s. He made his senior debut at just fourteen and soon established himself as the mainstay at the top of the order in a legendary side that included other Ireland internationals Ivan Anderson and the Harrison brothers Roy, Jim and Deryck.

Aged only nineteen he scored a century in the 1967 NCU Challenge Cup final against Muckamore, a feat he would repeat four years later in the 1971 final against Downpatrick.

His debut for Ireland came in what turned out to be perhaps the most famous match in the history of the game on the island when the West Indians were bowled out for just 25 at Sion Mills 1969. Reith had been drafted in to replace Dermott Monteith, who was forced to cry off due to work commitments, a strange piece of selection trading a left-arm spinner for a top-order batsman. In the event, Reith batted at No.3 and had the honour of hitting the runs (a push through cover) that registered Ireland's nine-wicket, first-innings victory. 'It was all quite surreal,' he recalled.

It was a terrific start to a fine forty-four-match career for Ireland that yielded 1,838 runs between 1969 and 1980. It would undoubtedly have been more but for a two-year spell in Australia, playing grade cricket in Sydney in 1973 and 1974.

His personal high point in Irish colours came against the Netherlands in 1970 when he struck a wonderful 129 in The Hague. It was to be his only century for Ireland, although he managed to pass 50 on eleven other occasions, not least during his final match against Scotland at Langloan, Coatbridge, in August 1980.

Having made his debut in Monteith's absence the pair became good friends, particularly on Ireland tours, as neither was afraid to let his hair down after matches. 'After I became captain, Michael installed himself as the unofficial shop steward of the team,' wrote Monteith in his book *A Stone from the Glasshouse*. 'He would make reasonable demands of the management but would also insist upon discipline and make sure players toed the line.'

Reith caused something of a stir in the early 1980s when he turned openly professional. Having won several NCU Challenge Cup and league titles with Waringstown he moved to the town of Comber where he became a professional player/coach with North Down CC, much to the disgust of many in the domestic game who felt it was a shame that the amateur ethos was being eroded. But despite enjoying a successful time at North Down, Reith's departure did not spark the feared wave of home-grown players to the professional ranks.

He retired from cricket in 1985 with back trouble and later took a job in leisure management with Banbridge council.

100 GREATS — Thomas Couland Ross
RHB, OB; Phoenix and Ireland (1894-1910)

According to Pat Hone, writing in 1955, Tom Ross was the greatest Irish bowler ever. He was an opening bowler with the ability to bowl quick inswing and offcutters, and was recognised in England when he was selected to play alongside Archie McLaren, Gilbert Jessop, CB Fry and Prince Ranjitsinjhi for the Gentlemen against the Players in 1902. The Gentlemen lost the game at Lord's by an innings and 68 runs, but Ross was not disgraced, return-ing figures of 28.5-6-76-2, taking the wicket of the great Wilfred Rhodes as the Players racked up 444.

Although born in Belfast, Ross was educated at Clongowes Wood in Co. Kildare, the hotbed of schools cricket in the late nineteenth century. He played his club cricket with Phoenix, and formed a devastating partnership with schoolmate Bill Harrington. He played only nineteen times for Ireland over seventeen summers, missing out on

Thomas Couland Ross
continued

Born: 14 February 1872, Belfast
Died: 2 January 1947, Foxrock, Dublin

Batting

Mts	Inns	NOs	Runs
19	31	2	491
Avg	50s	100s	Cts
16.93	2	-	21

Bowling

O	M	R	W
456.5	115	1258	86
Avg	5WI	10WM	
14.63	9	2	

Highest score: 89 v Scotland, College Park, 1910
Best bowling: 9-28 v South Africa, The Mardyke, 1904

the North American tours, but his 86 wickets came at less than 15 and featured several devastating returns.

His 9-28 against South Africa at the Mardyke in 1904 is still the best bowling for Ireland. On a day of glorious sunshine, he proved almost unplayable for the visitors. After Ireland made 160, Ross had an immediate impact, reducing South Africa to 11-3. Bill Harrington grabbed the fourth wicket but thereafter it was all Ross. 'It was a complete triumph for Ross, who has seldom if ever bowled better', wrote *The Irish Times*. 'Even allowing that the wicket gave him some assistance, it was a fine performance.' Ross was a master at varying his pace, and allied to a perfect length and some work on the ball, it is unsurprising that 'none of the batsmen seemed to be able to play him'.

He had made his debut against South Africa in 1894 – becoming the second bowler to take a wicket with his first ball for Ireland – but by the time they visited again in 1901 he had just five

caps. On his club ground he accounted for five of the top six in the order, finishing with 5-47. He was an automatic selection for Sir Timothy O'Brien's party for the maiden first-class tour of England the following May. He started the tour by clean bowling W G Grace, and ended it with 25 wickets, including 7-82 v MCC and 6-91 v Oxford University. His displays on tour earned him the call-up for the Gentlemen of England.

He never travelled abroad with Ireland thereafter, but was often the match winner against exalted visitors. He took six-for in each innings against Leveson-Gower's XI at Rathmines and seven in the match against the 1907 South Africans. He again accounted for Wilfred Rhodes when Yorkshire visited College Park in 1908. His last game for Ireland was against Scotland in 1910, aged thirty-eight, when he opened and made his career best 89. He was asked to play against South Africa in 1912 but was unfit. His batting was of all-rounder standard, most notably making 85 against Surrey at the Oval in 1895.

Edgar Donald Reid Shearer

RHB; City of Derry, NICC, North Down and Ireland (1932-52)

Born: 6 June 1909, Harrow-on-the-Hill, Middlesex.
Died: 9 July 1999, Sudbury, Suffolk, England.

Batting

Mts	Inns	NOs	Runs	
32	58	2	1300	
HS	**Avg**	**50s**	**100s**	**Cts**
102	23.21	8	2	27

Highest innings: 102 v Sir Julian Cahn's XI, 1937

Donald Shearer was an Englishman who made his home in Ireland, making a huge contribution to North-West and Irish sport, both on and off the field. He arrived in Derry straight from school at Aldenham to work in the textile industry. In April 1927 he made his debut with a 50 for City of Derry against Knockdara on a snowy pitch. After a modest couple of seasons he returned to England but came back to Derry in 1931 and scored 11 centuries in eleven years for the club. Shearer possessed every stroke in the book and was lightning-fast on his feet.

The hierarchies in Dublin and Belfast were dismissive of the North-West scene – no one had ever been capped from a NWCU club since Ireland started playing in 1855 – but when word seeped out of the feats of this talented youngster they couldn't ignore him. He first came to attention in 1928 when he was surprisingly selected for the province of Ulster XI to play the NCU President's XI in a charity match to showcase the great Australian player Charlie Macartney.

In 1932 it was presumed that he would be picked for Ireland but the Leinster branch objected that the rule that a player had to have played inter-provincial was being broken. The day before the selection meeting Shearer scored 80 in an hour off Boucher and Ingram and the objection was withdrawn! His debut against MCC was less successful but he made 73 at Lord's the following season and in the next fourteen games made 8 fifties and a century against Sir Julien Cahn's XI.

He had two excellent innings at Sion Mills in 1934: 59 for Ireland v MCC and 115 for the North-West against Lancashire. He continued to set records for City of Derry, most notably 233 v Killaloo and the first century in the North_West cup final.

He was the first to score 300 runs in a season for Ireland (1937) and one of his finest innings was for Ireland in College Park against the 1938 Australians, who included Bill O'Reilly. As wickets tumbled at the other end in the soft evening light, Shearer matched the great bowler with skill and elegance. No Irishman made double figures but Shearer used his feet to drive and glance and defied the 'Tiger' for three hours to make 56.

He was the first to score 50 in four successive innings in 1937 – 72, 52, 102, 52 – when he also became the first to score a century and fifty in the same game, against Cahn's XI.

During the war he served in the Middle East with the Royal Artillery and was mentioned in despatches and awarded an OBE at the end of the war. Afterwards he moved to Belfast and a successful business career, playing cricket for NICC and later North Down. He was less frequently available for Ireland and his international record was less notable after the war. All of his 8 fifties came pre-1939 but his final score of note came in August 1951, at the age of forty-two, when he made the first century for Ireland at Lord's. He captained Ireland nine times in 1946 and 1947.

When he first came to Ireland he played rugby for City of Derry but was spotted by Sir Dudley McCorkell, chairman of the newly formed Derry City and asked to join the soccer club. An amateur throughout his career, he arranged that if he was picked ahead of a professional player that the player would nonetheless be paid and receive the bonus if the team won.

As centre forward, Shearer played for Derry until 1939, scoring 78 goals, including 3 hat tricks in one season. He was a key player in the Irish League team which defeated the Football League in 1935 and 1936, the latter year also saw him capped for the English Amateur international team and the British Olympic side at the Berlin games. During his career he received a number of offers to turn professional, including one from Arsenal.

A successful businessman, he was appointed honorary ADC to the Governor of Northern Ireland in 1950 and from 1960 to 1969 he was ADC to the Queen. He was president of the ICU in 1966 and chairman of the NI Sports Council, and was appointed CBE in 1974 for his services to Northern Ireland. At the age of eighty-six he travelled to the 1996 ICU AGM in Dundalk to pay tribute to his recently deceased teammate and friend Jimmy Boucher.

John Francis Short

RHB; Cork Bohemians, Leinster and Ireland (1974-84)

100 GREATS

Like many Munster sportsmen down through the years, Jack Short was a brave, determined and proud operator who won admiration as much for the manner of his performances as for the statistics of his long and successful career.

Born in Cork and an alumnus of Presentation College and University College Cork, Short played at the Bohemians club until he moved for work reasons to Dublin in 1974, taking up membership of Leinster CC in Rathmines. A flamboyant opening batsman, Short actually made his debut for Ireland batting at No.3 as a twenty-three-year-old that year. In that game he instantly made a big impression, scoring 71 and 55 against the Netherlands at Amstelveen as Ireland won by three wickets.

At his best, he was a batsman who played with great fluency and he hated to be bogged down, no matter what the opposition. To him, the ball was there to be hit and the fact it had been sent down by Imran Khan, Wayne Daniel, Jeff Thomson or Joel Garner (as it was on occasion), meant little to the bearded Munster man. And this attitude was perhaps a weakness at times for there can be little doubt that with greater circumspection he would have scored more than his 2,515 career runs. He made 99 in the historic 1977 win over Sussex at Pagham before getting a good ball from Imran and there were several other disappointing dismissals including when he was on 33 and looking good during Ireland's first ever Gillette Cup match against

Born: 12 April 1951, Cork

Batting

Mts	Inns	NOs	Runs
56	91	5	2,515
Avg	**50s**	**100s**	**Cts**
29.24	15	3	34

Highest score: 114 v Scotland, Rathmines 1975

Middlesex at Lord's. Having seen off Daniel, Vincent van der Bijl, John Emburey and Mike Selvey, he got himself out to part-time bowler Mike Gatting.

He managed to pass the magic 100 mark on three occasions, a winning 114 against Scotland on a rain-affected Rathmines track in 1975, 104 against Wales at Pontardulais in 1981 and 103, also against Wales, at Rathmines the following year. There might have been another even more memorable century had Ireland not declared against the touring Australians in 1977 when Short was not out on 80. And that against a fired-up Jeff Thomson and Len Pascoe, who both seemed to be trying to knock his block off.

Without much of a throwing arm, Short carved out a niche for himself as an aptly named short-leg, taking a total of 34 catches for Ireland, many of them in that position. In 1979 he took six catches in a match against Wales at Marchwiel to equal the record held by Stuart Pollock.

A statistician by profession, Short's Ireland career ended early at the age of thirty-three when, as a civil servant, he was seconded to a post in Paris. He continued to play in his adopted country and even captained a France XI that defeated the MCC, but never added to his fifty-six Ireland caps thus depriving the country of his services at a time when he was still more than capable of performing at that level.

Writing at the end of Short's international career, respected former cricket correspondent for *The Irish Times*, the late Sean Pender said: 'He is one of those batsmen, like a Gooch or a Milburn on a larger stage, who stand out in their eras and dominate by their own special personality and brand of genius. He has that indefinable elegance and style given to so few batsmen, even to the most successful.'

Stephen Gordon Smyth
LHB; Brigade, Eglinton, Limavady and Ireland (1990-99)

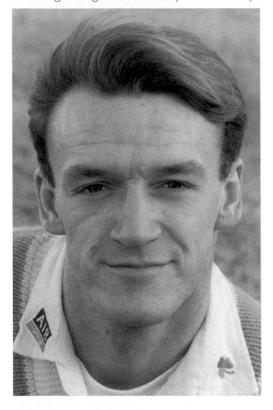

Born: 22 December 1968, Derry

Batting

Mts	Inns	NOs	Runs
64	76	10	1,912
Avg	50s	100s	Cts
28.97	10	1	29

Highest score: 102 not out v MCC, Pollock Park, Lurgan 1998

Along with Decker Curry, Stephen Smyth was one of the few North-West batsmen who was genuinely feared by any team he played against. He had the ability and fluency to take a match away from the opposition in a very short space of time.

A left-hander, Smyth was not as prolific a century-maker as Curry but was perhaps more technically correct with one of the finest cover drives in the Irish game. Indeed, playing for Ireland against Australia A in Castle Avenue one damp August day in 1998 he hit Andy Bichel for 5 fours through cover in one over, much to the annoyance of the Test fast bowler. Not surprisingly the sixth ball of the over wasn't quite so well pitched up and whistled past Smyth's ear.

'I think Smyth was probably the most correct batsmen from the North-West to play for Ireland,' said Barry Chambers of the CricketEurope website. 'At their peak, Curry

was probably a more destructive batsman and certainly scored a pile of runs but if you had to depend on someone to get a fifty for you, you might go for Smyth before Curry,' he said.

In total, Smyth played sixty-four times for Ireland, averaging just under 29 with the bat. His one and only century came against the MCC at Pollock Park, Lurgan, but he contributed several other wonderful innings prior to that, most notably 98 not out against the West Indies at Castle Avenue, Dublin, in 1995 facing the likes of Ian Bishop and Otis Gibson. He is also in the exclusive club of Irish internationals who have scored half-centuries on debut – he hit an unbeaten 59 against a Worcestershire side that included Ian Botham at Castle Avenue, Dublin in a one-day match in 1990. He captained Ireland on one occasion, a 17-run win over Wales at Paisley during the 1998 Triple Crown.

He has played for three clubs in the North-West – Eglinton, Brigade and Limavady – and continues to perform to a high standard with Limavady alongside Curry in what is a formidable batting line-up. It is probably fair to say that like most batsmen he would feel that he should have scored more runs. Often he would get to 50, whether for club or country, and then not go on to make a big score.

'But despite that flaw, he was a marvellous batsman, very compact with an excellent defence and he always seemed at ease, with plenty of time to play the ball. He was a terrific fielder too,' said Joe Doherty, former chairman of the Irish Cricket Union.

At times a fiery and controversial figure, he was banned from playing for Ireland for five years after a violent incident in Belfast's Stormont Hotel during a South Africa Cricket Academy tour in 1999, a decision that effectively ended his international career.

A good all-round sportsman, Smyth played many seasons of senior rugby in the All-Ireland League as scrum-half for City of Derry RFC. Indeed, he was dropped from the 1994 ICC Trophy squad to Kenya because he had turned out for City of Derry in a match against the orders of the ICU. Although quite short in stature, he had a strong upper body and was a tough competitor. There weren't many players who got the better of him in either his winter or summer sport.

100
GREATS

Robert George Torrens
RHB, RAM; Brigade and Ireland (1966-84)

Born: 17 May 1948, Derry

Batting

Mts	Inns	NOs	Runs
30	33	5	294
Avg	50s	100s	Cts
10.50	-	-	12

Bowling

O	M	R	W
643.3	138	1,976	77
Avg	5WI	10WM	
25.66	2	-	

Highest score: 44 v MCC, Lord's 1975
Best bowling: 7-40 v Scotland, Ayr 1974

Roy Torrens was a big-hearted, tall and ferocious opening bowler from the Brigade club in the North-West, who won thirty caps over an eighteen-year period from the late 1960s to the early 1980s.

A hugely popular character amongst his teammates, Torrens also had the respect of opponents who appreciated that he was a fearsome competitor on the field who enjoyed his cricket immensely but also someone who could leave it out on the pitch and enjoy a drink or two in good spirits afterwards.

One of the quicker bowlers to play for Ireland, Torrens used his extra height to achieve steep bounce and his stock ball was one just outside off stump, short of a length.

'The wickets in Ireland were not as good when Big Roy was playing as they are today and he was a truly lethal customer bowling on them with his pace and extra lift,' said former Strabane player and ICU chairman Joe Doherty.

'In those days, Roy was very fast. I'd love to know how many catches he had taken off his bowling at gully. Batsmen used to struggle as the ball steepled off a good length and they would lob catches off their gloves to Marshall Williamson, Torrens' teammate at Brigade,' said Doherty.

Torrens made his debut for Ireland in 1966 as a fresh-faced eighteen-year-old who turned up to play against Middlesex in Ormeau, Belfast, carrying his kit in a brown paper bag. He went out and took 4-77 that day but could not pre-vent Ireland losing by an innings and 21 runs to Fred Titmus and company.

His finest moment as an Irish player came in 1974 when he ran through a strong Scotland team at Ayr, bowling them out for just 91 and ending with figures of 7-40 in the first innings, going a long way to securing victory for Ireland by 52 runs.

'Two years later we went back on tour to that part of Scotland and they were still talking about it,' said Doherty.

In 1981, during a game against Surrey at the Oval, the Irish team had taken a dislike to the Kiwi Geoff Howarth who had expressed his displeasure at having to play in what he saw as a meaningless match. Then Irish captain Mike Halliday remembers the day well.

'It was coming to the end of the Irish innings and I asked Roy to go in and throw the bat and score a few quick runs,' said Halliday.

He faced his first ball which was a good length outside the off stump. He launched into an extravagant drive, missed the ball, followed through and the bat flew from his hands in the direction of Howarth, who was stationed at short leg. Luckily for him the bat sailed just over the Kiwi's head and also narrowly missed the square-leg umpire.

'When Roy returned to the visitors' changing room he announced: 'The skipper told me to throw the bat,"' said Halliday. To this day, Torrens denies he did it intentionally or that Howarth was the intended target but if he wanted to get rid of the close fielder, it was mission accomplished – Howarth did not stay long at short leg.

In that same game, Roy was taking a bit of a pasting from the Surrey openers, Alan Butcher and Duncan Pauline. In the third over of the innings as Halliday hastily reset the field with slips disappearing to all parts of the Oval, Torrens hesitated at the end of his run-up and shouted out that he would like 'Jacko' to move to the extra cover boundary. This would not normally be strange but for the fact that 'Jacko' (Paul Jackson) was the wicketkeeper. 'Well, he's not getting the ball where he is now,' roared Torrens to the con-siderable mirth of his teammates.

The thirty caps he won do not do justice to the talent of Torrens. In his early career he declined to play on the Sabbath out of respect for the wishes of his parents and throughout the time he was on the scene there was a plethora of quality opening bowlers with whom he had to compete for places, such as Alec O'Riordan, Dougie Goodwin, Podge Hughes, Simon Corlett, John Elder and Peter O'Reilly.

Although for Ireland he was very much a tail-end batsman, at club level he was an effective, hard-hitting, lower-order striker. In 1973 he bludgeoned 177 for Brigade against the Monroe attack in little over an hour and a couple of years later he dished out similar treat-ment to the Limavady bowlers, scoring 154 in no time at all.

The barrel-chested Torrens was also a tal-ented footballer, having played centre half for Ballymena United, Derry City and later he became player/manager for junior club Institute FC. In the late 1960s he captained a Northern Ireland amateur team that included Martin O'Neill, who went on to captain the senior side before launching his very successful manage-ment career in Britain.

In recent years the ever-popular Torrens has remained very much involved with Irish cricket, serving for several years as a national selector, president of the Irish Cricket Union and lately, manager for the national team.

Born: 24 May 1858, Forkhill, County Armagh
Died: 17 March 1912, Dublin

Batting

Mts	Inns	NOs	Runs
17	29	1	436
Avg	**50s**	**100s**	**Cts**
15.57	3	-	3

Highest score: 77 v MCC, Lord's 1879

According to the 1911 *Encyclopedia Britannica*, 'DN Trotter, who played for County Meath for many years towards the close of the nineteenth century, was a batsman who would have found a place in any English county eleven.' At his best he was the star Irish batsman of the nineteenth century, but he rarely showed signs of his teenage brilliance after he came of age.

Just a couple of weeks past his eighteenth birthday he scored 109 for Dublin University against the United South of England XI, the first century by an Irishman against professional opposition. Trotter was already an international, making his debut the previous August against I Zingari and remaining Ireland's youngest ever cap until Eoin Morgan, and later Greg Thompson, in the twenty-first century.

The son of a doctor, he was born in Co. Armagh but raised in Summerhill, Co. Meath, where he spent most of his life. He was educated in Dublin at Rathmines School and went up Trinity in 1872, aged fourteen years and two months. He was not yet sixteen when he made his debut and finished high up the averages. In 1875 he was awarded a record four presentation bats by the club – one each for scoring a fifty and a century against the United South of England and also for making 116 v Leinster and for topping the averages.

When he arrived in Trinity just two centuries had been scored in the club's forty years of existence; by the time he left he had made five more. His highest innings was 234 against Phoenix in

1877, when he put on 362 with Frank Kempster (128) for the second_wicket. Trotter stood erect at the crease and had powerful wrists, especially enjoying carving the ball on the up over point.

He never made a hundred for Ireland, his highest innings of 77 coming against MCC at Lord's in 1879. With Nat Hone making 87, the pair put on 161 for the first wicket, a record until 1992. While *The Times* said that Trotter deserved to be 'almost in the front rank' of batsmen, it complained the Marylebone had underestimated their opponents and the bowling wasn't up to scratch.

He got a chance to prove what *Britannica* asserted. His performances for Trinity were witnessed from mid-off by WG Grace and he put a word in so that Trotter was selected for the North of England in the annual match against the South at the Prince's Ground in 1877. WG was in his pomp and made 261 as the southerners won by an innings, but Trotter did not disgrace himself in making 9 and 33, dismissed on each occasion by Grace.

David North Trotter
continued

He went on the 1879 tour to the US and Canada, but had a poor run and was not selected again for four years. His recall came against I Zingari and he marked the occasion with a fifty. He was still good enough in 1889 to make 85 for a Trinity past and present selection against the Philadelphians and continued to turn out for Phoenix, Na Shuler and Co. Meath for many years. Pat Hone recalled a conversation with his father when he asked him what David did for a living, 'Nothing', he replied, 'he was a Co. Meath farmer'.

Deryck Andrew Vincent
LHB; Clontarf and Ireland (1986-91)

Born: 16 September 1964, Dublin

Batting

Mts	Inns	NOs	Runs
21	31	3	534
Avg	50s	100s	Cts
19.07	1	-	8

Bowling

O	M	R	W
4	2	11	-
Avg	5WI	10WM	
0.00	-	-	

Highest score: 52 not out v Wales 1988
Best bowling: 0-11 v Wales, Usk 1989

A quiet, diminutive and unassuming gentleman off the field, Deryck Vincent was capable of inspiring terror in the mind of any bowler as he strode out to the wicket with a bat in his hand. A left-hander with sweet timing of the ball, Vincent could dominate bowlers and quickly take the game away from the opposition.

While Vincent was one of the most feared players in Leinster club cricket for Clontarf CC, he never really replicated that on the international stage, possibly a psychological problem rather than one of ability. In a five-and-a-half-year career for Ireland he clocked up twenty-one caps, averaging almost 20 but only passing 50 once and never getting to a hundred. As a result he was never really an automatic choice for Ireland.

'He was probably one of the most devastating club batsmen I have ever played against,' said former Ireland captain and 121-times capped all-rounder Alan Lewis. 'He was quick on his feet, he was a great fielder and he could rip attacks apart with the bat but I always got the feeling that it was almost as if he didn't feel international cricket was his place. But of all the club batsman I played against, I probably feared bowling to him the most. He could thrash you anywhere in the ground. I had huge respect for him.'

Although not a strong man, Vincent had exquisite timing and generated fantastic bat speed through the ball. Like many smaller batsmen, he was able to move quickly and he was never slow in getting into position. He played the ball under his nose and was rarely beaten for pace, using the full depth of his crease to good effect.

He broke into the Ireland team in 1986 as a twenty-one-year-old when he was selected to tour Zimbabwe and he scored 36 runs in his first innings, putting on 76 runs for the third wicket with Mark Cohen as Ireland beat Matubeland by ten wickets at Bulawayo. He scored a 32 and a 21 later in that tour but, having made starts he was unable to push on, something that was a characteristic of his international career. Of his 31 innings for Ireland he passed 20 on 11 occasions but only managed one half-century, an unbeaten 52 against Wales in a drawn game at Castle Avenue in 1988. He felt that he wasn't always given a good chance by selectors and joked somewhat bitterly that he was the most-capped twelfth man for Ireland. Although only twenty-six in 1991, he decided to pack it in and concentrate on rugby, playing scrum-half for Dublin club Old Wesley in the All-Ireland League.

Perhaps Vincent's finest moment in his cricket career came a year after he had won his final cap for Ireland. Playing in the 1992 Leinster Senior Cup final against YMCA at the Phoenix Park, Vincent scored a magnificent 161 as Clontarf posted 338 for 6 off 60 overs, eventually winning the match by 44 runs. Vincent also took 5-72 with the ball making the man of the match award a simple choice. Although he ranks as one of the best batsmen in the history of Leinster cricket, his legacy is slightly tarnished by the fact that he never really replicated that form at the higher level.

100
GREATS

Laurence Warke
RHB, RM; Dublin University, Leinster, Woodvale and Ireland (1950-61)

Larry Warke was a belligerent batsman whose international career was something of a curate's egg. An average of 14.29 is very low for a man who had a decade-long career for Ireland, but in 34 of his 57 knocks he failed to reach double figures. Only eleven times did he pass 20, but on the two occasions he made a fifty he sailed past that mark and on past a hundred.

At Paisley in 1954, he made his maiden century against Scotland with 10 fours and 3 sixes, carting Willie Nicholl out of the ground. He was dropped at slip on 97, but brought up his hundred with another six off Jimmy Allan, the Kent and Warwickshire bowler.

He put on an opening stand of 104 with Stanley Bergin (26) but in the second innings made one of his eight international ducks. Captaining at Lord's three years later he made 1 as Ireland were bowled out for 92 by MCC, but second time around he was back to his brutal best making 101 to set a small target. He set his best bowling mark of 2-22 but defeat was inevitable. As captain he only tasted victory twice in eighteen games.

Warke was born in Belfast and educated at RBAI but he moved to Dublin in 1944 to study medicine at Trinity College. He made immediate impact for the university, and in one early fixture scored a rapid 70 against Clontarf, flaying an attack that included the celebrated Ireland bowler John Hill. At tea Hill was asked what he thought of this northern newcomer, 'he has one fault', he replied, 'overconfidence'. Warke marked his first Trinity tour with 112 against West of Scotland that July. While also playing with Woodvale in Belfast, he won league medals with the college in 1947 and 1948. In the latter year he played on the Woodvale sides that won the league and cup, and picked up another NCU Challenge Cup medal in 1949, scoring 46 in the final.

Born: 6 May 1927, Belfast
Died: 22 January 1989, Belfast

Batting

Mts	Inns	NOs	Runs
34	57	2	786
Avg	50s	100s	Cts
14.29	-	2	37

Bowling

O	M	R	W
191.1	33	644	13
Avg	5WI	10WM	
49.54	-	-	

Highest score: 120 v Scotland, Paisley, 1954
Best bowling: 2-22 v MCC, Lord's 1957

Nicknamed the Duke, he was one of a small number of men who made a thousand league runs for Trinity, making 1,156 including 6 fifties. As captain he made another rapid century against the Leprechauns in 1950, his 138 including 3 sixes, 1 five and 21 fours.

That was the year he was first picked for Ireland and despite his patchy record he missed only ten games in the following eleven years. To be fair to him, two-thirds of his games were on the poor Irish pitches of the era, where he averaged 12.3 – his average abroad was 18.2

He played several small but vital innings. In the centenary match against MCC in 1958, Ireland finished 15 short of victory on 82-9, with Warke's 32 the top score. He played his shots all around the wicket, with a slashing cover drive his most memorable stroke to one teammate. He was vulnerable early on but once he had the pace of the pitch and the measure of the bowling he was difficult to budge.

Until the mid-1950s he continued to play in the two unions, and he won cup medals with Woodvale in 1954 and Leinster in 1956 – scoring 114 against YMCA on the way to the final. He made a notable 111 out of 217 against Sion Mills in the 1957 cup. On returning to Belfast he took over as captain of Woodvale from 1958-62 and led them to a share of the league in his first season.

Stephen John Simon Warke
RHB, RAO; Woodvale and Ireland (1981-96)

Born: 11 July 1959, Belfast

Batting

Mts	Inns	NOs	Runs
114	151	10	4,275
Avg	**50s**	**100s**	**Cts**
30.32	28	4	54

Bowling

O	M	R	W
7	1	27	1
Avg	**5WI**	**10WM**	
27	-	-	

Highest score: 144 not out v Scotland, Castle Avenue 1985
Best bowling: 1-6 v MCC, Downpatrick 1992

Up to the time Stephen Warke won his first cap for Ireland as a twenty-one-year-old in 1981 the best-known player from the Woodvale club in Belfast was his father Larry, who won thirty-four caps in the 1950s and early '60s. But while he had a lot to live up to he soon surpassed his father's achievements in the Ireland sweater and became one of the finest batsmen of the modern era.

He ended up with 114 caps, putting him joint fourth on the all-time list and he is the only player to have scored more than 4,000 runs for Ireland (4,275 at an average of just over 30). But it nearly didn't happen for the big man as he struggled to establish a place in the team early in his career.

After making a creditable 33 in his first innings, against Canada at Ormeau, Belfast, Warke proceeded to score just four runs in his next four knocks, including three ducks. He played just once the following season and twice in 1983 but it was the second of those matches, against Scotland at Downpatrick, that marked the turnaround in his fortunes at that level as he made 63 and 45 as Ireland won by five wickets.

He had to wait nearly a year for his next cap, though, but when he hit 99 in the first innings at Ormeau against the MCC and 20 not out in the second, his days of being in and out of the side were over. He had made it and became perhaps Ireland's most consistent batsman of that era. Interestingly, that day Warke became the third Irishman to be dismissed on 99 at Ormeau and at that stage, no one had passed the magic three figures, a hoodoo finally beaten by Angus Dunlop in 1999.

In the face of a rapid and belligerent spell from Sylvester Clarke, Warke scored 77 while opening the batting against Surrey in the NatWest Trophy at a sun-drenched Oval later that season, winning him the man of the match award from former England Test player Trevor Bailey. And the following year he made an unbeaten 144 against Scotland at Castle Avenue, Dublin, his highest total in Ireland colours.

Warke was a level-headed and thoughtful cricketer who dominated club cricket in the Northern Cricket Union leagues and also put in several top performances in the Irish Senior Cup for Woodvale and the inter-provincial competition, then known as the Guinness Cup, for Ulster Town.

A stylish and elegant opening batsman, he was able to score all around the ground and through a feeling of solidity, particularly in defence, he gave a sense of security to those batting with him. He represented Ireland at various under-age levels from the time he was a schoolboy at Belfast Royal Academy and also played rugby with distinction at North of Ireland RFC.

He captained Ireland on thirty-nine occasions, winning just six matches with nineteen draws. He had been selected to skipper the team at Ireland's first ever appearance at the ICC Trophy in 1994 in Kenya but broke an elbow in a fielding accident just before the first match. An insurance broker by profession, he retired from representative cricket in 1996, leaving a considerable hole at the top of the Irish batting order.

Andrew Rowland White
RHB, RAO; North Down, Instonians, Northamptonshire and Ireland (2000-)

100 GREATS

Born: 3 July 1980, Newtownards, Co. Down

Batting

Mts	Inns	NOs	Runs
71	64	11	1,522
Avg	50s	100s	Cts
28.72	4	2	26

Bowling

O	M	R	W
371.3	27	1,708	63
Avg	5WI	10WM	
27.11	-	-	

Highest score: 152 not out v Netherlands, Deventer 2004
Best bowling: 4-28 v MCC, Lord's 2003

Known in the Ireland team as 'the finisher', Andy White has found himself at the crease for some of the most memorable victories in the history of the game in this country, and he has been not out in about one in five innings. He hit the winning runs as Ireland beat the West Indies by six wickets in Stormont in 2004 and was also there when they beat Surrey in the C&G Trophy the same season in Castle Avenue and the following year when they won the Intercontinental Cup final against Kenya in Namibia.

A hard-working player, White has never been one to throw his wicket away and has batted in every slot from two to eight as the need arose. He is always one who can raise his game for the big occasion. He made 152 not out in a first-class ICC Intercontinental Cup match against the Netherlands in Deventer during that memorable 2004 season and his best bowling came at Lord's a year earlier when he took 4-28 against the MCC.

He won a two-year contract at Northampton-shire as an off-spinning all-rounder where he was very much the type of player that Northants coach Kepler Wessels goes for: gritty, deter-mined, industrious and without a hint of ego. But despite these qualities his bowling didn't progress as much as it should have and he never established himself in the first team. In fact, some would argue that his game went downhill during his time at Northants and certainly his confidence seemed to take a pounding as he was consistently left out of the first team.

The fact that he was not a mainstay for Northants meant that he was usually available for his country and his willingness to fulfil any role within the team that was asked of him was a big plus. He can do all three disciplines of bat-ting, bowling and fielding well and although he is a quiet character on and off the field, his vital contributions for Ireland when the chips were down, speak volumes for his dedication and mental strength. White's father Rowland can be seen at most Ireland games, sitting behind a huge camera lens, taking the action pictures to adorn the pages of newspapers, magazines, programmes and websites associated with the game.

'Andy is a dependable players and the sort of approachable team man that makes my job as coach so much easier,' said national coach Adrian Birrell. 'No matter what he is asked to do on the field, he does it with a great attitude and, as we have seen time and again, he usually does it very, very well.'

Other titles published by Nonsuch

Literary Walking Tours of Gothic Dublin
BRIAN J. SHOWERS

Dublin has spawned three important writers in the nineteenth-century gothic tradition: Charles Maturin, Joseph Sheridan Le Fanu, and Bram Stoker. This guidebook reconstructs the lives of these writers as walking tours with the help of maps, photographs and excerpts from their works. Reprinted inside are Maturin's 'Leixlip Castle', Le Fanu's 'Ghost Stories of Chapelizod' and Stoker's 'The Judge's House'.

1 84588 523 6

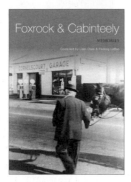

Foxrock and Cabinteely
EDITED BY LIAM CLARE AND PÁDRAIG LAFFAN

Compiled by the Foxrock Local History Club and edited by Liam Clare and Padraig Laffan, long-term residents recount their memories of 'old times' and newer residents tell their tales of settling into the changing communities.

1 84588 527 9

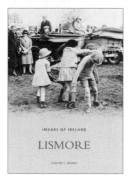

Lismore
EUGENE DENNIS

Founded in the seventh century by St Carthage, Lismore takes pride in its history and traditions. This collection of over 200 images, many of which are published here for the first time, recalls aspects of everyday life, including, work, education, sport and the arts.

1 84588 501 5

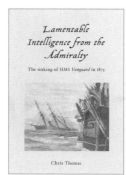

Lamentable Intelligence from the Admiralty
The Sinking of the HMS Vanguard in 1875
CHRIS THOMAS

HMS Vanguard sank in thick fog in Dublin Bay in September 1875, rammed by her sister ship. Chris Thomas examines what happened, setting it in context and highlighting the outcome including the unjust conclusions of the Court Martial and the tragic effect on Captain Richard Dawkins and his family.

1 84588 544 9

If you are interested in purchasing other books published by Nonsuch, or in case you have difficulty finding any Nonsuch books in your local bookshop, you can also place orders directly through our website
www.nonsuch-publishing.com